# Suicidal Thoughts

## Essays on Self-Determined Death

Edited by
Max Malikow

*Contributors: A. Alvarez, Olive Ann Burns,
Sue Chance, Earl Grollman, Eric Hoffer, Kay Jamison,
Gordon Livingston, Max Malikow, Karl Menninger,
Sherwin Nuland, Walker Percy, Rick Reilly,
Edwin Shneidman, Rod Steiger, William Styron,
and Judith Viorst*

**Hamilton Books**
A member of
The Rowman & Littlefield Publishing Group
*Lanham • Boulder • New York • Toronto • Plymouth, UK*

**Copyright © 2009 by**
**Hamilton Books**
4501 Forbes Boulevard
Suite 200
Lanham, Maryland 20706
Hamilton Books Acquisitions Department (301) 459-3366

Estover Road
Plymouth PL6 7PY
United Kingdom

Library of Congress Control Number: 2008927838
ISBN-13: 978-0-7618-4118-0 (paperback : alk. paper)
ISBN-10: 0-7618-4118-0 (paperback : alk. paper)
eISBN-13: 978-0-7618-4201-9
eISBN-10: 0-7618-4201-2

∞™ The paper used in this publication meets the minimum
requirements of American National Standard for Information
Sciences—Permanence of Paper for Printed Library Materials,
ANSI Z39.48—1984

To SC: Who has looked into the depths of life and retained her grace. I admire you.

To Kay Jamison: Who understands suicide thoroughly and whose book, *Night Falls Fast*, is the finest ever written on the subject.

To William Styron: Who suffered, yet favored us with poignant stories— including his own.

# Contents

# Foreword

The book you are about to read provides a unique view of the world of suicide. It is a world inhabited by people who have committed or contemplated suicide and those who live in its devastating aftermath. The writings collected here are authored by a variety of accomplished professionals woven together by the happenstance of personal experience. Struggles of selfhood, debilitating depression, and existential longing take the reader (or at least this reader) to an inside corner of the self where our fears about life and death cling to the fragile props of our own invention. It is a testimony to Max Malikow's long devotion to understanding suicide, as well as his editorial acumen, that this book grabs our hearts for both the questions it makes us consider and the people it helps us to understand.

This collection of essays brings us into the soul of suicide's compelling power to destroy or transform those within its grip. It is the heart of suicide from *inside* the world of those who live and breathe the possibility or reality of suicide. It is a world where the heart's lament sings loudly and cries for relief. We are privileged to enter here and to bear witness to the celestial and the secular tug of life and death. These authors write with their hearts and allow us a glimpse into their sacred struggle.

I am reminded of Mary Catherine Bateson's (1990) masterful book, *Composing a Life*, where she explores the notion that accomplished lives are not the product of singular ambition, but rather an "improvisational life form" or composition created by life's interruptions and detours, the arrivals of joy and the pain of departure. The monologues presented in the essays you are about to read are improvisation of the highest form that turn the suicidal prism around so that we can see suicide's many faces—an escape, a mercy, a crucible, a crucifixion, a resurrection, and, sometimes, a redemption.

Marie DiTullio, Ed.D.,
Associate Professor of Psychology
Le Moyne College

# Preface

A wise and helpful professor once advised me to locate the "fire that burns within" for the topic of my doctoral dissertation. He reasoned that since I would be immersed in that topic for several years, it should be one that would sustain my interest. I opted for suicide and, fifteen years after the completion of my dissertation, I confess to giving disproportionate attention to suicide in the courses I teach as well as gravitating toward suicidal patients in my clinical work. Why? Perhaps Camus is right: "There is but one truly serious philosophical problem, and that is suicide. Judging whether life is or is not worth living amounts to answering the fundamental question of philosophy" (1955).

Years of studying suicide have reassured me that I am not alone in my desire to understand this truly serious philosophical and psychological problem. I am indebted to a variety of writers who have provided me with insight into the subject. With this volume, it is my pleasure to share some of their thoughts with you.

Max Malikow
Syracuse, New York
June 26, 2007

# Acknowledgments

When I was invited to present on suicide at the Wesleyan Medical Center in Wichita, Kansas in the summer of 2007, I did not realize it was the start of a project that would culminate as a collection of essays for publication. Without Cindy Harmon's invitation, this volume would not exist.

A quotation that introduces one of the essays in this anthology comes from Thomas Merton: "My first human act is the recognition of how much I owe everybody else." I am indebted to Maria DiTullio, Earl Grollman, and Edwin Shneidman for the encouragement and suggestions they provided for this project.

I am grateful for the work of each of the contributors to this book. Editing this anthology reacquainted me with some of the most fluent writing ever accomplished on the complex subject of suicide.

Finally, I acknowledge Dr. James A. Manganello for his commitment to excellence in the field of clinical psychology.

# Permissions

# Introduction

*Death means we can finally retire and just be still, quiet, unmasked of, without demands or tomorrows, allowed to sleep. The absolute, final tranquilizer—how could that not be seductive?*

—Edmund Spenser

I recently prepared for a conference on suicide by rereading two of the finest books on the subject: Kay Jamison's *Night Falls Fast* and Edwin Shneidman's *The Suicidal Mind*. I do not know the number of books that address suicide, but after thirty years of reading about self-administered death, I know there are many. So why one more?

This book is the result of an attempt to compile some of the most moving and insightful writing accomplished on the subject of suicide. Such an anthology must include the thoughts of the aforementioned Jamison and Shneidman as well as A. Alvarez, Eric Hoffer, Karl Menninger, Sherwin Nuland, and William Styron. The controversial psychiatrist Thomas Szasz wrote:

Suicide is a fundamental human right. That does not mean that it is morally desirable. It only means that society does not have the moral right to interfere, by force, with a person's decision to commit this act (1973, p. 67).

In contrast to Szasz, the philosopher Immanuel Kant believed that people have a duty to live, regardless of their circumstances. He reasoned that life is sacred because it is part of nature and people are obligated to preserve their unique place in the natural order. Kant believed it praiseworthy for people to rise above their despair and persist in life in the face of adversity.

The reader who is seeking a moral argument for or against suicide would be better served to read elsewhere. There is little in this volume that addresses suicide as an ethical issue. The purpose of this collection is to present the thoughts of fifteen writers who have contemplated suicide—some profession-ally, others personally, and, a few, both personally and professionally. This col-lection is intended for anyone—mental health professional, suicide survivor, suicide contemplator—who desires to have a better understanding of why some people give serious consideration to killing themselves. This collection will help the reader to appreciate the complexity of suicidal thinking.

## Chapter I

# Sylvia Plath: A Miscalculation?

## A. Alvarez

*A. (Alfred) Alvarez, is an English poet and former poetry editor and critic of "The Observer." His treatise on suicide,* The Savage God, *includes the following speculation that the suicide of celebrated poet, Sylvia Plath, was a cry for help that went awry.*

> *The woman is perfected.*
> *Her dead*
> *Body wears the smile of accomplishment . . .*
> *Her bare*
> *Feet seem to be saying:*
> *We have come so far, it is over.*
> —Sylvia Plath, "Edge"

Around six o'clock in the morning, she went up to the children's room and left a plate of bread and butter and two mugs of milk, in case they should wake hungry before the *au pair* girl arrived. Then she went back down to the kitchen, sealed the door and window as best she could with towels, opened the oven, laid her head in it and turned on the gas.

The Australian girl arrived punctually at nine o'clock. She rang and knocked a long time but she could get no answer. So she went off to search for a telephone booth in order to phone the agency and make sure she had the right address. Sylvia's name, incidentally, was not on either of the doorbells. Had everything been normal, the neighbor below would have been up by then; even if he had overslept, the girl's knocking should have aroused him. But as it happened, the neighbor was very deaf and slept without his hearing aid. More important, his bedroom was immediately below Sylvia's kitchen. The gas seeped down and knocked him out cold. So he slept on through all

1

the noise. The girl returned and tried again, still without success. Again she went off to telephone the agency and ask what to do. They told her to go back. It was now about eleven o'clock. This time she was lucky: some builders had arrived to work in the frozen-up house, and they let her in. When she knocked on Sylvia's door there was no answer and the smell of gas was overpowering. The builders forced the lock and found Sylvia sprawled in the kitchen. She was still warm. She had left a note saying, "Please call Dr. ____" and giving his telephone number. But it was too late.

Had everything worked out as it should—had the gas not drugged the man downstairs, preventing him from opening the front door to the *au pair* girl—there is little doubt she would have been saved. I think she wanted to be; why else leave her doctor's telephone number? This time, unlike the occasion ten years before, there was too much holding her to life. Above all, there were the children: she was too passionate a mother to want to lose them or them to lose her. There were also the extraordinary creative powers she now unequivocally knew she possessed: the poems came daily, unbidden and unstoppable, and she was again working on a novel about which, at last, she had no reservations.

Why, then, did she kill herself? In part, I suppose, it was a "cry for help" which fatally misfired. But it was also a last desperate attempt to exorcise the death she had summed up in her poems. I have already suggested that perhaps she had begun to write obsessively about death for two reasons. First, when she and her husband separated, whether she was willing or not, she again went through the same piercing grief and bereavement she had felt as a child when her father, by his death, seemed to abandon her. Second, I believe she thought her car crash the previous summer had set her free; she had paid her dues, qualified as a survivor and could now write about it. But as I have written elsewhere, for the artist himself, art is not necessarily therapeutic; he is not automatically relieved of his fantasies by expressing them. Instead, by some perverse logic of creation, the act of formal expression may merely make the dredged-up material more readily available to him. The result of handling it in his work may well be that he finds himself living it out. For the artist, in short, nature often imitates art. Or, to change the cliché, when an artist holds up a mirror to nature he finds out who and what he is; but the knowledge may change him irredeemably so that he becomes the image. . . .

I suspect that in the end she wanted to have done with the theme once and for all. But the only way she could find was "to act out the awful little allegory once over." She had always been a bit of a gambler, used to taking risks. The authority of her poetry was in part due to her brave persistence in following the thread of her inspiration right down to the Minotaur's lair. And this psychic courage had its parallel in her physical arrogance and carelessness. Risks didn't frighten her; on the contrary, she found them stimulating. Freud has written: "Life loses in interest, when the highest stake in the game of living, life itself, may not be risked." Finally, Sylvia took that risk. She gambled for the last time, having worked out that the odds were in her favor, but perhaps, in her depression, not much caring whether she won or lost. Her calculations went wrong and she lost.

It was a mistake then, and out of it a whole myth has grown. I don't think she would have found it much to her taste, since it is a myth of a poet as a sacrificial victim, offering herself up for the sake of her art, having been dragged by the Muses to that final alter through every kind of distress. In these terms, her suicide becomes the whole point of the story, the act which validates her poems, gives them their interest and proves her seriousness. So people are drawn to her work in much the same spirit as *Time* magazine featured her at length: not for the poetry but for the gossipy, extraliterary "human interest." Yet just as the suicide adds nothing at all to the poetry, so the myth of Sylvia as a passive victim is a total perversion of the woman she was. It misses altogether her liveliness, her intellectual appetite and harsh wit, her great imaginative resourcefulness and vehemence of feeling, her control. Above all, it misses the courage with which she was able to turn disaster into art. The pity is not that there is a myth of Sylvia Plath, but that the myth is not simply that of an enormously gifted poet whose death came carelessly, by mistake and too soon.

*Chapter II*

# Uncle Camp's Suicide

## Olive Ann Burns

*Olive Ann Burns (1924–1990) wrote* Cold Sassy Tree *over a nine-year period, starting when she was diagnosed with cancer. Published in 1984, it was an immediate bestseller that has retained its popularity to the present. A journalist, she wrote for the* Atlantic Journal *under the pseudonym Amy Larkin. "Cold Sassy Tree" is the name of a small town in Georgia. The story is told by Will Tweedy, a fourteen year-old boy. Here is his account of the suicide of another of the book's characters—the gloomy Campbell Williams.*

> *You can outdistance that which is running after you, but not what is running inside you.*
>
> —Rwandan proverb

> *Most men lead lives of quiet desperation and go to the grave with the song still in them.*
>
> —Henry David Thoreau

Uncle Camp got away from Aunt Loma while she was gone to Athens. She had caught the train that Saturday morning, wearing a black wool dress and the big hat with ostrich plumes that Miss Love had made. She was to spend the day with her LaGrange College roommate, Sue Lee Gresham, who was now Mrs. Humphrey Wright of Athens.

Uncle Camp had gone to work early that day, and since Papa thought that any lady taking a train should have somebody see her off, he told me to drive Aunt Loma to the depot. To my mind she didn't need a ride any more than if she was going downtown, which she did every day, and besides, she was leaving Campbell Junior with Mama and Queenie. And naturally I wasn't too crazy about being alone with her. She might take the occasion to raise cain about the Christmas play. But Papa said to, so I went and got her.

She was far from friendly, but her mind was on Athens, not me or rats.

Aunt Loma really didn't want to go, or so she said as we waited at the depot. "Sue Lee's just usin' me as an excuse to have a luncheon. She hopes I'll be jealous of her. She always writin' about her big house and her big dinner parties, and her husband bein' president of the bank. I don't call inheritin' a bank from your daddy any proof that you're smarter than the next fellow." Aunt Loma stepped back from the tracks as the train came in sight. "I just wish I hadn't told her I'd come."

I always thought ladies liked being honor guests at a luncheon, and I said so. "Besides, ain't nobody makin' you go."

"Camp made me," she said, real irritable.

"Well, I be-dog." Chalk up one for ole Camp.

"He promised to fix the faucet in the bathtub if I'd just get out of his way. Said he couldn't tackle the job with me standin' there watchin' him fail."

Poor ole Camp.

Papa said afterwards that Camp actually applied himself that morning at the store. Instead of waiting around to be told what to do, he put in a real good morning's work. And whereas he usually had about as much life in his eyes as a turtle, he seemed almost happy.

He and my daddy left together at dinnertime. On the way out the door, camp asked Papa would he mind stopping by the house before going back to the store after dinner. Kind of apologetic, like he hated to take up Papa's time, he explained. "I'm fixin' to fix a leaky faucet, Mr. Hoyt, and I ain't never done one. I'd shore feel better if you'd come to see did I do it right. I . . . well, you know how Loma is.

Papa did stop by, though grudging. I was with him. The door was open, despite it was a cold day, and we went on in. "Camp?" Papa called.

"I'm in the kitchen, Mr. Hoyt. Come on back, hear?"

The shot rang out about time Papa set foot in the dining room. Neighbors said they heard somebody scream. It must have been me or Papa, though later I couldn't recall anything except the smell of gunpowder and, on the floor, a big long blob of blue and white checked oilcloth. He had laid down on a length of it, pulled up one end over him like a sheet and the other end down over his head and chest, and after calling Papa to come on back, had put the pistol in his mouth and pulled the trigger.

I reckoned he figured if all the blood and bits of bone and brains got trapped in the oilcloth, Loma baby wouldn't be mad at him.

Papa lifted the part that was over Camp's head, put it down quick, and turned away, his face like ashes. I had seen, too. I stood there, shaking. Finally I said, "Papa, want me to run get Doc Slaughter?"

He could hardly speak. "Run, get Mr. Birdsong, son."

Mr. Birdsong offered me a ride up beside him in the driver's seat of an old horse-drawn hearse, the one he called an ambulance if the person wasn't dead. Since the neighbors were already gathering, he drove the horses around to the back door, where my daddy was waiting. Papa had closed the kitchen door and hadn't let anybody go in there.

Mr. Birdsong tied up Camp in that oilcloth as if he were a dern side of beef. Me and Papa helped carry him out, and rode with him to the big old white-columned funeral parlor.

Mr. and Mrs. Birdsong and their nine children lived upstairs. Helping take Uncle camp in there, I wondered how they could stand to live like that with dead bodies, especially when it was one that had committed suicide.

Papa hurried home to tell Mama and sent me to the store to tell Grandpa and them, but they had already heard. As I ran in, Grandpa met me at the door, grim of face. He asked me a few questions, then stalked off to the funeral parlor.

Soon as I could get away from the customers who pressed around, asking more questions, I ran back to Aunt Loma's. I wanted to make sure there wasn't any blood or anything on the floor.

If there was, Mrs. Brown next door had cleaned it up. But I could still see Uncle Camp, same as if he was laying right there with his brains blowed out, and it made me sick. I felt about to faint. Leaving the kitchen, I rushed past the people whispering in the hall and went to the bathroom.

I nearly stumbled over the plumbing tools. Uncle Camp had left them on the floor by the tub.

Just what you'd expect, Camp not putting up his tools.

Then I saw a piece of paper stuck under the big wrench. I knew it was for Aunt Loma, but horses couldn't of kept me from reading it.

You can get the creeps, I tell you, reading what a dead man has just written. This is what it said.

Loma baby, I tried to plan so as not to mess up yr kitchen.
i loved you since the day i laid eyes on you jus as pretty now
as then. So it ain't you Loma baby its I ain't good for nuthin.
which you know. Its got so jus getin out of bed in the
morning is to much. I pact up my close and all in a box so
you wouldn have to fool with it. My leavin this werl don't
have nuthin to do with you bein mad at me for not fixin the
fawsit I been aimin to do it a long time fore the fawsit went to leekin.

plese save my gold pockit watch for Campbell Junior
i leeve it to him I aired it from my grandedy you know. I
love you an always will but now you can have some pese.
tell mr. Blakesly I preshate him givin me the job like he done
now he can fine him somebody who can do him a good dase work
  i hope god will forgive me so I can meet you in heven.
  plese don't be mad I have plan it so you wont be the one to fine me.
    yr lovin husban Campbell Williams.
p.s. i fix the fawsit
p.s. i wont to be berit in cold sassy so you can vist me some time.
Yr lovin husband Campbell Williams.

The page blurred. I wish so bad I could of known Uncle Camp for the past three years like I knew him now that he was dead. But even as I stood there holding his sweet and lonely words, I heard the water going *drip, drip, drip* into the bathtub.

I picked up the wrench and changed the washer. Nobody was go'n say Campbell Williams was so sorry that he couldn't even fix a faucet. It was a small thing to do for a man brave enough to put a pistol in his mouth and shoot.

*Chapter III*

# A Survivor's Benediction

## Sue Chance, M.D.

*Sue Chance's son, Jim, committed suicide at age twenty-five by a self-inflicted gun shot.*

*Her deeply moving story is told in* Stronger Than Death: When Suicide Touches Your Life. *"A Survivor's Benediction" is taken from the final chapter of her book.*

> *O my son Absalom! My son, my son Absalom! If only I had died instead of you—*
> *O Absalom, my son, my son!*
> —King David, 2 Samuel 19:3

I remember my astonishment when I heard Edwin Shneidman say at the 1987 American Association of Suicidology meeting that suicide is consistent with the rest of the suicide's life. Those who commit suicide typically didn't handle past disturbances well, have a very limited capacity to endure psychological pain, and have a penchant for constriction (a kind of narrowed perspective), black and white thinking, and running from their problems.

Fits Jim to a tee. Does it pain me to admit that? Yes, it does. But it would pain me more to go on believing that his choice was driven by *my* mistakes and shortcomings. The questions are not, What did I do wrong and what should I have done differently? They are, Why did he persist in things that didn't work and why would he not go for help or accept it when it was offered? Those questions are unanswerable, of course, but then so were the original ones. The ones about him are simply more to the point.

Needless to say, I got very, very angry at Jim. I was in a towering rage the whole third year of my bereavement. But gradually a tempering process set in as I realized more and more that, in an ironic way, Jim was considerate. He spared even those he was angriest at from finding his body: and that is a *ma-*

*jor* trauma to survivors. I can only imagine the horror of seeing the mutilated body of someone you love. I listened to Mariette Hartly describe the suicide of her father in the next room and watched as she gestured helplessly, saying, "And, I cleaned my father's"—she was too overcome for a moment to continue, but we all filled in the blanks, knowing the unspoken words were—"brains off the wall."

I amplified my agony at first, visualizing that moment and its immediate consequences. My medical training was a kind of curse, since I could very adequately imagine that through-and-through explosion of his beloved head. However, I soon realized that persisting in those images was a sure path to madness, and when I caught myself doing it, I'd scold myself, saying, "Just knock it the hell off, Sue." Believe it or not, that was effective. Incidentally, there is a name for that technique—it's called thought-stopping and it's exactly what it sounds like. By hook or by crook, you make yourself change the subject. Most survivors could stand to do it more often.

You have to go by way of anger. It's intrinsic to the survival process. Only by doing it can you begin to experience forgiveness—of the suicide and of yourself. It's like one of those monsters of the mind that is always gaining on you in your dreams. You have to face it if you're ever going to stop running.

I want to remind you of something I said earlier in this book: you don't know what anyone else is feeling unless he or she tells you. . . . The thing I've come to realize is that I can't understand Jim's pain any more than he could have predicted mine. I don't know what I meant to him. He didn't know what he meant to me. Even those closest to us remain an enigma in many ways.

I also believe that, whatever failures of a parent or parents, at some point the individual takes over his or her own destiny. In working with adolescents from very sick families, I finally decided that the best thing I could do is give them the following lecture: "You want to tell me how much your parents have messed up and how much pain they've caused you. I believe you. I know that your complaints are legitimate. But you're coming closer and closer to the time in your life when you can take over and make it better for yourself. That's going to be your choice: whether you stay stuck in blaming and moaning about all the things which have been unfair or get on with it and do the best you can with what you have."

Kids don't like that message any better than adults do, any better than I did the first time I gave it to myself. But it has the utility of being true and ultimately helpful.

I do not like my parents and I do not like the things they did to me. However, I am responsible for who I am now. There is no way I can reasonably say that, at forty-nine, I am more a product of the first fifteen years I spent with them than I am of the past thirty-fours years spent with myself. I would, in fact, be very ashamed of myself if it were true.

We are all a work in progress. Life isn't about getting everything right. It's about adapting, about learning to love the sorrows of our changing faces. Suicide short-circuits that. It is not only an untimely end but a failure of adaptation and growth. As Shakespeare said in *Othello*, "How poor are they that have not patience! What wound did ever heal but by degrees?"

The suicide doesn't wait around for that healing. His survivors have to believe that it's coming or they will commit suicide themselves. And there are a myriad of ways to do that—drugs and alcohol, emotional isolation, living in a fantasy, to name a few. If, on the other hand, they want to live and heal, they have to acknowledge that it is the suicide who bears the ultimate responsibility. Accepting this enables them to pick up the threads of their own lives and relationships and go on with them.

There have been changes in how I view death and how I view life. Much remains a mystery, but I know more about loss and resolution than most people. I know how to survive. I know how to be strong. I know how to love. . . .

He rejected his life, but I can't. I must use his life to master my own. And perhaps that mastery will be a form of creation.

Mastering and creating ourselves is a lifelong task. In order to do it, we must hold fast to that enduring, abiding love that embodies the universal good. Our love for others and for ourselves comes from and returns to that source.

That source is where my son has gone.

And I believe that source is stronger than death.

## Chapter IV

# A Suicide Occurs—The Abuse
# of Religion

### Rabbi Earl A. Grollman, D.D.

*Rabbi Grollman has written twenty-eight books and over one-hundred articles on death, dying, and bereavement. In the following essay, he provides a summary of centuries of philosophical and theological thought concerning suicide.*

> *If you can force your heart and nerve and sinew*
> *To serve your turn long after they are gone,*
> *And so hold on when there is nothing in you*
> *Except the Will which says to them, "Hold on!"*
> —Rudyard Kipling, "If"

I often speak before community groups on the subject of suicide. After the conclusion of the talk, it is not unusual during the coffee break for attendees to share their personal, intimate experiences. (Perhaps the subject of a future article could be on the topic of responding to a throng of people whose complex problems cannot possibly be addressed in terse simplistic answers under these conditions. I now refer them to a professional in their own area or suggest they telephone me at a later date when there are not time restrictions and together we can truly discuss in-depth issues.)

On multiple occasions their problem revolves not only upon them as suicide survivors but the lingering aftermath of the funeral. There are the emotional repercussions of the bereaved: heartache, anger, shame, and recrimination. There is an additional dimension! At the worship, the clergy may transform the eulogy (meaning "praise") into a brutal attack upon the suicide. "He is guilty of self-murder!" "She is now burning in the fiery furnace of hell!" The language not only directly stigmatizes the dead but the survivors who are indirectly held accountable and responsible by church and synagogue for the heinous "transgression."

# SUICIDE AMONG EARLY PHILOSOPHERS

People have been killing themselves since the beginning of recorded history. Attitudes toward suicide have varied from age to age and civilization to civilization.

In the First Egyptian Period (2000 B.C.), there is the famous dialogue of the man who was consumed by such unendurable pain and torment that he contemplated taking his life. There is no intimation of violation of the Egyptian spiritual or legal code.

Stoicism, the school of philosophy in Athens about 300 B.C., believed that "when circumstances made existence no longer bearable, one could voluntarily withdraw from life by suicide." A Roman stoic who believed he "had enough life" had his veins severed by trained technicians. Epicurus (350 B.C.) pronounced: "Death is nothing to us, because when we are, death is not. When death is, we are not." Cato (50 B.C.), Pliny (110 A.D.), and a host of others concurred.

In contrast, there were dissenters who condemned the act of suicide. Plato said: "Only one thing I know, that it is better if need be to suffer the extreme of injustice." The Greek philosopher Socrates (390 B.C.) together with the poets Virgil (19 B.C.) and Ovid (18 A.D.) argued that suicide was never morally justified.

Society tended to react in a hostile manner (with some noticeable exceptions) against self-inflicted death. Some thinkers asserted that the manner in which a person departs from life reflects not only one's philosophy of life but a possible contempt for the group as well. The theologian Thomas Aquinas (1225-74 A.D.) argued that suicide robbed the community of one of its integral parts. An individual had the duty to live even against his or her own wishes because of obligations to the group. The German philosopher Immanuel Kant (1788) summed it up: "Suicide is an insult to humanity." How different from the earlier Roman philosopher Lucius Seneca (4 B.C.–65 A.D.) in his Epistle 70: "The wise man will live as long as he ought, not as long as he can . . . It is not a question of dying earlier or later, but dying well or ill. And dying well means escape from the danger of living ill."

# SUICIDE AMONG EARLY RELIGIONS

With almost the first words of Genesis: "And God saw all that he had made, and found it very good," a Jewish thesis is stated: Life is good and must be treasured.

Despite a religious emphasis upon the sanctity of life, the Hebrew Holy Scriptures contain but six sporadic references to self-destruction. In each case there are extenuating circumstances, such as the fear of being taken captive or the possibility of suffering humiliation or unbearable pain.

Jews first came to regard suicide as taboo with Flavius Josephus (ca. 37–100 A.D.), one of their great historians. (These sentiments were later echoed in the daughter religions, Christianity and Islam.) The ancient Israelites were intensely concerned for the survival of their tiny nomadic group, and regarded suicide of even one Hebrew as a threat to tribal community.

In Talmudic times (200–500 A.D.), an increasing number of suicides is recorded. The rise is partly due to spiritual and social crises, partly due to a growing Greco-Roman influence. Now that the act had become more frequent, a condemnatory tone is injected. It is stated that the self-homicide forfeits his or her share in the world-to-come and shall be denied burial honors. The Talmud decrees that suicides are to receive no eulogy or public mourning. They are to be buried apart, in community cemeteries with attendant public shame for survivors.

When Christianity came into being, suicide was very common in Greece and Rome. The early Christians apparently accepted the prevailing attitudes of their era, particularly when persecution made life unbearable. Many early Christians submitted to Roman torture and allowed themselves to be killed as martyrs. Suicides in this period, whether direct or indirect, were based on the eagerness to do away with the misery of the world in order to experience the joys of immortality. The Apostles did not denounce self-execution; the New Testament touched on the question only indirectly in the report of Judas' death. For several centuries the leaders of the church did not condemn this widespread practice.

Until Augustine (354–430 A.D.) denounced suicide as sin, there was no official church position against it. After deliberating at great length whether self-imposed death could be condoned in the case of a woman whose honor was in danger, Augustine asserted it could not, for "suicide is an act which precluded the possibility of repentance, and is a form of homicide and thus a violation of the Decalogue Article, 'Thou shalt not kill.'"

The earliest organizational disapproval of suicide was expressed by the Second Council of Orleans in 533. Churches were permitted to receive offerings on behalf of those who were killed in the commission of a crime provided they did not lay violent hands on themselves. Suicide was regarded as one of the most serious of transgressions. In 563 the Fifteenth Canon of the Council of Braga denied the suicide funeral rites of the Eucharist and the singing of psalms. The Council of Hereford in 673 withheld burial rites to those who died through self-destruction. In 1284, the Synod of Nimes refused suicides interment in holy ground.

A further and perhaps more refined elaboration of the Augustinian concept was expounded by Thomas Aquinas who opposed suicide on three postulates: (1) it was against the natural inclinations of preservation of life and charity toward the self; (2) suicide was a trespass against the community; and (3) it was a trespass against God, who had given humankind life. For Saint Thomas, all life was a preparation for the eternal. His argument stressed the sacredness of human life and absolute submission to God.

For Islam, suicide was considered one of the greatest sins, the violation of *Kismet*. The faithful Moslems await their destiny; they do not snatch it from the hands of God. Suicide is expressly forbidden in the *Koran*.

## SUICIDE AND MORE MODERN THEOLOGIANS

Jewish sages realized that there were certain extenuating circumstances under which the rigid restrictions and prohibitions about suicide could be waived. Joseph Karo (1488-1575), perhaps the most outstanding of legal authorities, said: "Without proof to the contrary, a person is not pronounced to be wicked. If therefore an individual was discovered to be hanged or choked, as far as possible the act of killing should be regarded as the deed of another person and not his own deed." What about a minor? "If a minor committed suicide, it is considered that he had done the deed unwittingly." The matter was approached from the standpoint of mental illness: "If adults killed themselves and it is evident that the act was prompted by madness, they shall be treated as ordinary diseased people." Although considered a crime against God, suicide could sometimes be explained away, understood, and forgiven. In later years, many Jews committed suicide while in the Nazi concentration camps awaiting to be slaughtered. Controlling the time of their death was an affirmation of the victims' freedom.

In modern Judaism, there is both understanding and compassion concerning those who take their lives. Suicides are afforded all the honors and rites usually granted to the dead, thus sparing surviving relatives additional disgrace. Those who commit suicide are generally regarded as emotionally distressed and overwrought and therefore not responsible for their actions. Rabbi Yeheil Michel Epstein expressed these sentiments over eighty years ago in his influential code *Arukl Hashulchan*: "In regard to suicide, we find whatever circumstances we can to remove the person who has apparently committed suicide from the denial of mourning rites."

Most Christian groups today are outraged when the suicide is denounced by clergy as "burning in the fiery furnaces of hell." The situational, or contextual, ethics of Anglican theologians like Joseph Fletcher and John Robinson represent a change from the attitude of absolute condemnation. They argue that the question of suicide is an open one that must take into account the particular situation, the uniqueness of each human relationship, and the distinctiveness of each person. As Bishop Robinson suggests: "Truth finds expression in different ages."

Today, many clergy view the question of suicide not only from the theological level, but also consider the deep psychological causes and sociological implications. Ethical-religious approaches are counterbalanced with the broader perspectives of the social sciences. Increasingly, suicide is being recognized not only as a religious question but as a major medical problem.

For this reason, denominations such as the Anglican church, taking into consideration modern research, appointed commissions to revise the harsh religious laws regarding suicide. The Lutheran church in America does not regard suicide as an "unforgivable sin" and Lutherans who take their own lives are not denied a Christian burial.

In the Catholic Church, a directive was issued to priests in the Archdiocese of Boston relative to Canon 1240 of the Code of Canon Law, which forbids Christian burial to "persons guilty of deliberate suicide . . ." The late Cardinal Cushing interpreted the law in this way:

> The Church forbids Christian burials to suicides, but only if they were in full possession of their faculties at the time of the crime. The element of notoriety must be present in a suicide for the penalty to be incurred. Hence, no matter how culpable it may have been, if it is not publicly known that the act was fully deliberate, if the culpability is known only to a few discreet people, burial is not to be denied. Ordinarily, there is not too great a difficulty in granting Christian burial to a suicide, since most people these days consider the fact of suicide to be a sign of at least temporary insanity.

For these reasons, former Bishop Thomas J. Riley of St. Peter's Catholic Church in Cambridge stated that he could not recall a single case in Massachusetts of Christian burial being denied a suicide.

## A SUICIDE

In the Koran, suicide is forbidden. Among some Muslims, heroic or altruistic suicide is encouraged. Acts of self-destruction can be performed on behalf of God and country. One need only view the faces of young people of the

Middle East who use their bodies in a mood of exultation to detonate enemy mines. By intentionally taking their lives on behalf of Allah, there will be greater rewards in the world-to-come.


## CONCLUSION

Virtually all faiths agree that the mystery of God-given life is the greatest gift of all. There is a reverence for life and patience in suffering.

At the same time, we remember Thornton Wilder's *The Bridge of San Luis Rey*, when a bridge collapses and plunges the persons crossing it to their deaths. In an attempt to discover what it was in each person's life that brought him or her to the ill-fated bridge of self-destruction, Wilder enunciated one certain truth: "There is the land of the living and a land of death and the bridge is love—the only survival, the only meaning."

In our tumultuous and alienated world, it is the death of love that evokes the love of death. That is why it is mandatory that the faith community extend *continuing* love, support, and understanding to suicide survivors—to help (not hinder) their ability to build a temple of tomorrow's dream in the grave of yesterday's anguish. How dare we victimize and stigmatize those who remain! Before one offers words and actions that would, recall the sage: "Do not judge your neighbor until you are in his or her place."

## Chapter V

# A Philosopher
# Almost Commits Suicide

## Eric Hoffer

*Eric Hoffer (1902–1983) lived a unique life. Blinded in an accident at age seven, his sight inexplicably returned at fifteen. Fearing that his sight would again leave him as suddenly as it had returned, he resolved to read as much as he could for as long as he could. He retained both his sight and his appetite for books for the rest of his life. His life ranged from being a homeless indigent to an internationally recognized philosopher and recipient of the Presidential Medal of Freedom. The best known of his ten books is* The True Believer. *The following narrative from his memoir,* Truth Imagined, *recounts his decision to commit suicide.*

> *Tomorrow and tomorrow and tomorrow creeps in this petty pace from day to day.*
>
> —Macbeth, V.5.

As the end of 1931 approached, the time came to decide what I would do when the money was gone. Actually, my mind was already made up: I would commit suicide. All I had to do was settle the details. I had to find the means of a quick, painless death. A revolver would have been ideal, but it was not to be had without a police permit. Gas might leak into adjoining rooms and alarm the neighbors. Death by jumping from a bridge or being run over seemed crude. There remained poison. The article on poison in the *Encyclopedia Britannica* gave me all the information. The corrosive poisons, such as carbolic acid, which are the salts of heavy metals, act slowly and cause much pain. The abrasive poisons, such as oxalic acid, are more subtle. They penetrate into the bloodstream. But they also attack the intestines and cause vomiting. The systemic poisons, such as potassium cyanide, affect the nervous system and bring about unconsciousness. They act rapidly and cause little pain. The same is more or less true about strong opiates such as Veronal. A round of several drugstores showed that no potassium cyanide was to be had. Veronal and other opiates were sold only on doctor's orders. I settled therefore on oxalic acid. The encyclopedia mentioned it as a common cause of accidental poisoning, since its crystals resembled those of Epsom salt, which has a wide use as a bleach. I bought a large quantity of oxalic acid for twenty-five cents. Thus in one day my task was done.

My last day was Sunday. From the moment of waking I was conscious of a dark worry hammering on my brain. It dominated the room. The books on the table, the pots and plates in the corner did not meet my eye with the joyful familiarity of the days before. They looked like visiting friends who came inopportunely on a family quarrel; they turned their backs. What had happened? It was not the fact that I was to die in the evening, for death had no image or voice which on closer approach I could see or hear and be gripped with fear. Even as late as the small hours of the preceding night my mind was peaceful. I was rereading for hours the tales of Jacob and his sons chuckling over the vivid details and marveling at the unsurpassed storytelling. Now I was like one lost in a dark forest; I dared not leave my bed. Thus, between gray drowsing and gloomy waking, I passed the hours until the black night raised itself to my window and beckoned me to come out. In retrospect, it is clear that the reason for the sudden worry that morning was simply the disappearance of a "tomorrow." Death would have been no terror were it to come a month from now, a week, or even a day. For death's one terror is that it has no "tomorrow."

I poured the oxalic crystals in a bottle half full of water. Part of it dissolved and the rest settled on the bottom. I wrapped the bottle in a newspaper and went out into the street. My intention was to walk out beyond the city, where any cries of anguish would find no response, and if, driven by pain, I would rush back for help it would be of no avail, for a run of two miles or so would accelerate the working of the poison and put an end to all efforts.

I followed Figueroa Street southward. The bright sidewalks eased my mind. The restaurants were crowded. Waiters in uniforms fluttered about the tables and behind the counters. The clank of silver and the call of orders escaped into the warm night. Streetcars buzzed back and forth; they seemed like huge lanterns suspended from a wire. At a stopping place a middle-aged man and a boy were waiting for a streetcar. They were in the full light of a street lamp. I saw the boy raising himself on tiptoe to adjust the tie of the older man and to smooth the lapels of the dark suit, and all the while the boy talked eagerly. When done, he clasped the hand of the older man again and stamped his feet with joyous impatience.

Away from the center of the city the sidewalks were deserted. The small restaurants, far apart, were gathering places for the neighborhood families. Here and there brilliantly lit vegetable markets were glittering islands in the vast darkness.

I adjusted the bottle against my arm and thought feverishly, "It would be good if this street had no end—I would walk on forever, and my feet would never tire; neither would I fret, nor complain." I thought of roads winding through green fields and orchards, running out to the blue ocean. There seemed nothing so pleasant as walking on roads, legs and hands swinging, and the knapsack rocking gently. I did not know then that the vision of life as an endless road was the first intimation of a revulsion against suicide.

By now I was walking on a dirt road. Oil derricks like gibbets suddenly loomed ahead of me. A tall eucalyptus tree stood alone in the field to the left of the road. I made for it, stumbling over rough ground. My thoughts ran on feverishly while I freed the bottle from its wrappings. I removed the stopper and took a mouthful. It was as if a million needles pricked the inside of my mouth. In a blaze of anger I spat the oxalic acid out, continued spitting and coughing, and while wiping my lips I let the bottle fly and heard its thud in the dark.

I hastened back to the road, still spitting and coughing. I ran on the dirt road, I reached the cement paving. The sound of my steps on the paved road was like the clapping of hands. I was in a fever of excitement and talked to myself. I kept running until I joined the crowd. The lamps, the flashing traffic signals, the ringing bells, the streetcars, the automobiles, all the handiwork of man seemed part of my flesh and bone. I walked toward the cafeteria tingling with a ravenous appetite.

As I swallowed my food the vision of life as a road—a winding, endless road that knows not where it goes and what its load—came back to me. Here was an alternative I had not thought of to the deadening routine of a workingman's life in the city. I must get out on the road which winds from town to town. Each town would be strange and new; each town would proclaim itself the best and bid me take my chance. I would take them all and never repent. I did not commit suicide, but on that Sunday a workingman died and a tramp was born.

*Chapter VI*

# The Pact

## Kay Jamison, Ph.D.

*Kay Redfield Jamison is a Professor of Psychiatry at the Johns Hopkins University School of Medicine. One of the world's foremost authorities on suicide, her books include her best selling memoir,* An Unquiet Mind, *and* Touched with Fire: Manic-Depressive Illness and the Artistic Temperament. *"The Pact" is an excerpt from* Night Falls Fast: Understanding Suicide.

> *Whensoever any affliction assails me, methinks I have the keys to my prison in my own hand, and no remedy presents itself so soon to my heart as my own sword.*
>
> — John Donne, *Biathantos*

Summer evenings at the Bistro Gardens in Beverly Hills tended toward the long and languorous. My friend Jack Ryan and I went there often when I lived in Los Angeles, and I invariably ordered the Dungeness crab and scotch on the rocks. Not so invariably, but time to time, Jack would use the occasion to suggest we get married. It was an idea with such patent potential for catastrophe that neither of us had much of an inclination to take the recurring proposal with too much gravity. But our friendship we took seriously.

This particular evening, having hooked and tugged out the last bits of crab, I found myself edgily knocking the ice cubes around in my whiskey glass. The conversation was making me restless and uneasy. We were talking about suicide and making a blood oath: if either of us again became deeply suicidal, we agreed we would meet at Jack's home in Cape Cod. Once there, the nonsuicidal one of us would have a week to persuade the other not to commit suicide; a week to present all the reasons we could come up with for why the other should go back on lithium, assuming that having stopped it was the most likely reason for the danger of suicide (we both had manic-depressive illness and, despite the better and often expressed judgment of others, had a tendency to stop taking lithium); a week to cajole the other into a hospital; to invoke conscience; to impress upon the other the pain and damage to our families that suicide would inevitably bring.

We would, we said, during this hostage week, walk along the beach and remind the other of all the times we had felt at the end of hope and, somehow, had come back. Who, if not someone who had actually been there, could better bring the other back from the edge? We both, in our own ways and in our own intimate dealings with it, knew suicide well. We thought we knew how we could keep it from being the cause of death on our death certificates.

We decided that a week was long enough to argue for life. If it didn't work, at least we would have tried. And, because we had years of cumulative experience with lifestyles of snap impetuousness and knew how quick and final a suicidal impulse could be, we further agreed that neither of us would ever buy a gun. Nor, we swore, would we under any circumstances allow anyone else to keep a gun in a house in which we lived.

"Cheers," we said in synchrony, ice and glass clinking. We sealed our foray into the planned and rational world. Still, I had my doubts. I listened to the details, helped clarify a few, drank the rest of my scotch, and stared at the tiny white lights in the garden around us. Who were we kidding? Never once, during any of my sustained bouts with suicidal depression, had I been inclined or able to pick up a telephone and ask a friend for help. Not once, it wasn't in me. How could I seriously imagine that I would call Jack, make an airline reservation, rent a car, and find my way out to his house on the Cape? It seemed only slightly less absurd that Jack would go along with the plan, although he, at least, was rich and could get others to handle the practicalities. The more I thought about the arrangement, the more skeptical I became.

It is a tribute to the persuasiveness, reverberating energies and enthusiasms, and infinite capacity for self-deception of two manic temperaments that by the time the dessert soufflés arrived we were utterly convinced that our pact would hold. He would call me; I would call him; we would outmaneuver the black knight and force him from the board.

If it has ever been taken as an option, however, the black knight has a tendency to remain in play. And so it did. Many years later—Jack had married and I had moved to Washington—I received a telephone call from California: Jack had put a gun to his head, said a member of the family. Jack had killed himself.

No week in Cape Cod, no chance to dissuade. A man who had been inventive enough to earn a thousand patents for such wildly diverse creations as the Hawk and Sparrow missile systems used by the U.S. Department of Defense, toys played with by millions of children, and devices used in virtually every household in America; a Yale graduate and lover of life; a successful businessman—this remarkably imaginative man had not been inventive enough to find an alternative solution to a violent, self-inflicted death.

Although shaken by Jack's suicide, I was not surprised by it. Nor was I surprised that he had not called me. I, after all, had been dangerously suicidal on several occasions since our Bistro gardens compact and certainly had not called him. Nor had I even thought of calling. Suicide is not beholden to an evening's promises, nor does it always hearken to plans drawn up in lucid moments and banked in good intentions.

I know this for an unfortunate fact. Suicide has been a professional interest of mine for over twenty years, and a very personal one for considerably longer. I have a hard-earned respect for suicide's ability to undermine, overwhelm, outwit, devastate, and destroy. As a clinician, researcher, and teacher I have known or consulted on patients who hanged, shot, or asphyxiated themselves; jumped to their deaths from stairwells, buildings, or overpasses; died from poisons, fumes, prescription drugs; or slashed their wrists or cut their throats. Close friends, fellow students from graduate school, and children of colleagues have done similar or the same. Most were young and suffered from mental illness; all left behind a wake of unimaginable pain and unresolvable guilt.

Like many who have manic-depressive illness, I have also known suicide in a more private, awful way, and I trace the loss of fundamental innocence to the day that I first considered suicide as the only solution possible to an unendurable level of mental pain. Until that time I had taken for granted, and loved more than I knew, a temperamental lightness of mood and a fabulous expectation of life. I knew death only in the most abstract of senses; I never imagined it would be something to arrange or seek.

I was seventeen when, in the midst of my first depression, I became knowledgeable about suicide in something other than an existential, adolescent way. For much of each day during several months of my senior year in high school, I thought about when, whether, where and how to kill myself. I learned to present to others a face at variance with my mind; ferreted out the location of two or three nearby tall buildings with unprotected stairwells; discovered the fastest flow of morning traffic; and learned how to load my father's gun.

The rest of my life at the time—sports, classes, writing, friends, planning for college—fell fast into a black night. Everything seemed a ridiculous charade to endure; a hollow existence to fake one's way through as best as one could. But gradually, layer by layer, the depression lifted, and by the time my senior prom and graduation came around, I had been well for months. Suicide had withdrawn to the back squares of the board and became, once again, unthinkable.

Because the privacy of my nightmare had been of my own designing, no one close to me had any real idea of the psychological company I had been keeping. The gap between private experience and its public expression was absolute; my persuasiveness to others was unimaginably frightening.

Over the years, my manic-depressive illness became much worse and the reality of dying young from suicide became a dangerous undertow in my dealings with life. Then, when I was twenty-eight years old, after a damaging and psychotic mania, followed by a particularly long and violent siege of depression, I took a massive overdose of lithium. I unambivalently wanted to die and nearly did. Death from suicide become a possibility, if not a probability, in my life.

Under the circumstances—I was, during this, a young faculty member in a department of academic psychiatry—it was not a very long walk from personal experience to clinical and scientific investigation. I studied everything I could about my disease and read all that I could find about the psychological and biological determinants of suicide. As a tiger tamer learns about the mind and moves of his cats, a pilot about the dynamics of the wind and air, I learned about the illness that I had and its possible end point. I learned as best I could, and as much as I could, about the moods of death.

*Chapter VII*

# A Psychiatrist's Son Commits Suicide

## Gordon Livingston, M.D.

*Dr. Livingston is a graduate of West Point and the Johns Hopkins School of Medicine. He has practiced psychiatry since 1967. Awarded the Bronze Star for valor in Vietnam, he is the author of three books. In his national bestseller,* Too Soon Old, Too Late Smart *(Avalon Publishing, 2004) he wrote about his son's bipolar illness and eventual suicide.*

> *While the child was still alive, I fasted and wept . . . But now that he is dead, why should I fast? Can I bring him back again? I will go to him, but he will not return to me.*
>
> —2 Samuel 12:22,23

And what is psychotherapy? It is goal directed conversation in the service of change. That's what people who come for help want: *change*. Usually they want to alter the way they're feeling: anxious, sad, disoriented, angry, empty, adrift. Our feelings depend mainly on the interpretation of what is happening to us and around us – our attitudes. It is not so much what occurs, but how we define events and respond that determines how we feel. The thing that characterizes those who struggle emotionally is that they have lost, or believe they have lost, their ability to choose those behaviors that will make them happy.

Think about a person so disabled by worry that he can no longer function comfortably in the world. Every decision must be measured against the probability that it will increase or decrease anxiety. To the degree that one's choices become constrained by a need for anxiety avoidance, one's life shrinks. As this happens, the anxiety is reinforced and soon the sufferer becomes fearful, not of anything external, but of anxiety itself. People become afraid to drive, to shop, sometimes even to leave their houses. At this point some patients feel their choices in life have become so constricted that they withdraw from human contact. This same withdrawal can be seen in severe depression.

When confronted with a suicidal person I seldom try to talk them out of it. Instead I ask them to examine what it is that has so far dissuaded them from killing themselves. Usually this involves finding out what the connections are that tether that person to life in the face of nearly unbearable psychic pain. There is simply no denying the anger embedded in any decision to kill oneself. Suicide is a kind of curse forever on those who love us. It is, to be sure, the ultimate statement of hopelessness, but it is also a declaration to the ones closest to us that their caring for us and our caring for them was insufficient to the task of living through another day. People in despair are, naturally, intensely self-absorbed. Suicide is the ultimate expression of this preoccupation with self. Instead of just expressing the sympathy and fear that suicidal people evoke in those around them, therapists included, I think it is reasonable to confront them with the selfishness and anger implied in any act of self-destruction.

Does this approach work to prevent someone from killing himself? Sometimes. In thirty-three years of practicing psychiatry I have lost this argument only once. A young mother of two, going through depression triggered by a bitter divorce, shot herself on the day she was to enter the hospital. When she didn't appear I met the police at her house and found her body. Whatever fantasies I had entertained about being able to control the life of another despairing human being left me that day.

And then, many years later, I received a phone call telling me that my precious son, Andrew, age twenty-two, had ended his three year struggle with bipolar illness by killing himself. Even now, thirteen years later, words cannot contain the grief that has been my constant companion since that awful day. It is an offense to the natural order of life for parents to bury their children. In a just world it would never happen; in this world it does.

When Andrew surrendered his long fight with despair, he left behind so many people who loved him and whose memories encompass an intermingling of the joy he brought to us and the eternal sadness of his death. When I inventoried the record of his life that he left with me, I came across a school essay that he had written when he was nine. It read, in part:

*It was about 2:30 PM and my father and I had been running for over an hour. We were now heading into the wind so I got behind my father and he broke the wind for me. We were competing against 200 other runners. It was a hard course with many steep hills. In the last mile we increased the pace and passed several runners. When we reached the track, we had to go half way around it, and then we finished the thirteen mile race.*

He was a wonderful student, president of his high school class, and had been elected to the student council as a sophomore at college when he was gripped by the first symptoms of his illness. He endured three hospitalizations and his moods oscillated wildly between manic disorganization and grinding depression. I imagine that his final desperate moments were eased with some anticipation of release from the anguish he had endured. I pray that he found at last the peace that he sought.

His illness proved a cold wind that none of us could shield him from, and in the end it swept him away. He chose the too-soon moment of leaving, but I know he loved us as we loved him, and I have forgiven him my broken heart, believing that he forgave me all mistakes as his father. When I remember his laugh I hear the lyrics of an old Tom Paxton song:

> *Are you going away with no word of farewell?*
> *Will there not be a trace left behind?*
> *I could've loved you better,*
> *Didn't mean to be unkind.*
> *You know that was the last thing on my mind.*

## Chapter VIII

# Altruistic Suicide

## Max Malikow, Th.D.

*Max Malikow is a psychotherapist and on the faculty of Syracuse University's Renee Crown Honors Program. His books include* Living When a Young Friend Commits Suicide *(Beacon Press, 1999), co-authored with Rabbi Dr. Earl Grollman, and* Profiles in Character *(University Press of America, 2007).*

> *Greater love has no one than this, that he lay down his life for his friends.*
> — The Gospel of John 15:13

For well or ill, my daughter's early childhood included a father who was writing a doctoral dissertation on suicide. When she was five she asked the inevitable question, "Dad, what is suicide?" I told her that suicide is the word for when someone decides to die and then does something to make it happen.

"Oh," she responded, "you mean like Jesus?"

The French sociologist Emile Durkheim classified suicide into four categories, one of which he designated *altruistic suicide* (Durkheim, 1897). Self-sacrifice is the defining feature of this type of suicide. Durkheim characterized altruistic suicide as the opposite of *egoistic suicide,* in which there is an extreme sense of self and no sense of obligation to others. An altruistic suicide is a self-determined death motivated by what is perceived as a service to another person or other persons. This essay provides a description of three lethal actions taken by individuals for the sake of others.

In her bestselling memoir, *An Unquiet Mind,* psychologist Kay Jamison provides this moving description of a childhood memory.

The noise of the jet had become louder, and I saw the children in my second-grade class suddenly dart their heads upward. The plane was coming in very low, and then it streaked past us, scarcely missing the playground. As we stood there clumped together and absolutely terrified, it flew into the trees and exploded directly in front of us. . . . Over the next few days it became clear, from the release of the young pilot's final message to the control tower before he died, that he knew he could save his own life by bailing out. He also knew, however, that by doing so he risked that his unaccompanied plane would fall onto the playground and kill those of us who were there. . . . The dead pilot became a hero, transformed into a scorchingly vivid, completely impossible ideal for what was meant by the concept of duty. . . . The memory of that crash came back to me many times over the years, as a reminder both of how one aspires after and needs such ideals, and how killingly difficult it is to achieve them. (Jamison, 1995, pp. 12–13).

In 1995 a headline in *The Washington Post read:* "Mother picks death to continue her life through son's birth." The story that followed was that of a mother who chose to forego the aggressive treatment of her cancer that would have aborted her baby.

Clementine Geraci, three months pregnant, made the decision of her life when doctors told her last spring that her breast cancer had spread. She could fight the cancer aggressively and have an abortion, or she could take the less hazardous cancer drugs and carry the baby to term. . . . Geraci, known as Tina, died Monday, March 6, at Washington Hospital Center, where she worked as a resident in obstetrics and gynecology. She was 34. . . . During most of her pregnancy, Geraci took taxol, which doctors thought would not harm Dylan (her son). She had to stop taking the drug in the seventh month of her pregnancy, and Dylan was born one month prematurely by Caesarean section, during which doctors discovered cancer in her liver. She resumed treatment, but it was too late (*The Washington Post*, March 7, 1995).

In *The Pursuit of Happiness* psychologist David Myers provides the following narrative.

With Nazi submarines sinking ships faster than the Allied forces could replace them, the troop ship *SS Dorchester* steamed out of New York harbor with 904 men headed for Greenland. Among those leaving anxious families behind were four chaplains, Methodist preacher George Fox, Rabbi Alexander Goode, Catholic priest John Washington, and Reformed Church minister Clark Polling. Some 150 miles from their destination, a U-456 caught the *Dorchester* in its cross hairs. Within moments of a torpedo's impact, reports Lawrence Elliot, stunned men were pouring out from their bunks as the ship began listing. With power cut off, the escort vessels, unaware of the unfolding tragedy, pushed on in the darkness. On board, chaos reigned as panicky men came up from the hold without life jackets and leaped into overcrowded lifeboats.

When the four chaplains made it up to the steeply sloping deck, they began guiding men to their boat stations. They opened a storage locker, distributed life jackets, and coaxed men over the side. In the icy, oily smeared water, Private William Bednar heard the chaplains preaching courage and found the strength to swim until he reached a life raft. Still on board, Grady Clark watched in awe as the chaplains handed out the last life jacket, and then, with ultimate selflessness, gave away their own. As Clark slipped into the waters he saw the chaplains standing—their arms linked—praying, in Latin, Hebrew, and English. Other men, now serene, joined them in a huddle as the *Dorchester* slid beneath the sea (Myers, 1992, p. 196).

## CAN A SUICIDE BE ALTRUISTIC?

Professor Daniel Robinson is among those who have pondered the question: Is an act of undiluted altruism even a possibility (Robinson, 2007)? Those who maintain that altruism is a concept without a corresponding reality have argued that every act of benevolence is tainted by self-interest. They would posit that if Mother Teresa experienced satisfaction from obedience to her calling and joy in her work, then her concern for others was mixed with self-gratification. Further, it is possible that she carried on her laudable work without any sense of self-sacrifice.

Such reasoning is specious. *Altruism* is defined as "concern for the welfare of others, as opposed to egoism" (*American Heritage Dictionary*, 1973). There is nothing in this definition that suggests altruistic acts must be unadulterated. It is significant that *altruism* is in common usage and readily understood. It is a word that describes the spirit in which an act is performed.

The philosopher Ayn Rand has posited that altruism's actual existence does not establish it as a virtue.

> Altruism holds *death* as its ultimate goal and standard of value—and it is logical that renunciation, resignation, self-denial, and every other form of suffering, including self-destruction, are the virtues it advocates. And, logically, these are the only things the practitioners of altruism have achieved and are achieving now (Rand, 1964, pp. 37–38).
>
> The Objectivist ethics holds that *human* good does not require human sacrifices and cannot be achieved by the sacrifice of anyone to anyone. It holds that the *rational* interests of men do not clash—that there is no conflict of interests among men who do not desire the unearned, who do not make sacrifices nor accept them, who deal with one another as *traders*, giving value for value (p. 34).

However intellectually appealing Rand's position might be, consider your visceral reaction to the pilot, Tina Geraci, and the four chaplains. Do you consider their actions deserving of commendation or condemnation? It is selflessness—not egoism—that is the ubiquitous virtue. Can you think of a culture that recognizes and honors absolute self-preservation and simultaneously derides actions like the three that are cited in this essay?

## WHAT MOTIVATES AN ALTRUISTIC SUICIDE?

A suicide can be motivated by a sense of duty. The Indian practice of suttee in which the widow at a Hindu funeral could express her devotion to her husband by throwing herself on the pyre was a dutiful suicide. (This ritual was outlawed under British rule in 1826.) Americans became familiar with another form of suicide in the line of duty during World War II when Japanese kamikaze pilots intentionally flew their explosive laden planes into targets. The term *kamikaze* came from the combination of the Japanese words for divine or God (*kami*) and wind (*kaze*).

A self-determined death can be motivated by love. When Jesus spoke the words, "Greater love has no one than this, that he lay down his life for his friends" (John 15:13), he was anticipating his crucifixion. Jesus also spoke of his imminent death as part of his mission and therefore his duty: "Now my heart is troubled, and what shall I say? 'Father, save me from this hour?' No, it was for this very reason that I came to this hour" (John 12:27).

The psychologist Lawrence Kohlberg's *moral stages theory* consists of six stages of moral reasoning ranging from simplistic and concrete to abstract and principled. Stage six moral reasoning is characterized by what an individual personally perceives as unqualified ethical principles. The United States Marine Corps motto, "Death before dishonor" and its Japanese Samurai warrior counterpart, seppuku, are military ethical principles that place honor above the preservation of life. Obedience to these codes of conduct could result in death in the line of duty as well as death on behalf of a comrade.

## ARE THE THREE SELF-DETERMINED DEATHS PRESENTED IN THIS ESSAY ALTRUISTIC SUICIDES?

Words have both definitions and usages; the former are found in dictionaries and the latter in lexicons. The three aforementioned deaths meet the criteria for *suicide* (the act or instance of intentionally killing one's self) and *altruistic* (characterized by a concern for the welfare of others as opposed to one's own).

History speaks favorably of those who have sacrificed their lives for others. In the Gettysburg Address, Abraham Lincoln honored soldiers who gave their "last full measure of devotion" (Lincoln, 1863). During the Battle of Britain, Winston Churchill expressed his nation's debt to the pilots of the Royal Air Force with the words: "Never in the field of human conflict was so much owed by so many to so few" (Humes, 1995, p. 123). The Reverend Dr. Martin Luther King went so far as to say, "I submit to you that if a man hasn't discovered something that he will die for, he isn't fit to live" (King, 2008).

## IF ALTRUISTIC SUICIDES EXIST, ARE THEY MORALLY RIGHT ACTIONS?

Ethical philosophy has two general categories of ethical systems: *teleological* and *deontological*. Derived from the Greek word for "end" (*telos*), a teleological approach to ethics determines moral right and wrong in terms of the desired goal. In the case of the Air Force pilot, his goal was to avert a tragedy. By staying with the plane, it did not crash in the schoolyard. Therefore, teleologically, he did the right thing. The same can be said of Tina Geraci. If the goals of the four chaplains were to save lives other than their own, actualize their faith, and encourage men facing imminent death, then the chaplains displayed moral uprightness.

Derived from the Greek word for duty (*deon*), a deontological approach to ethics measures rectitude in accordance with ethical principles or code of moral conduct. Deontologically, the pilot, Tina Geraci, and the four chaplains showed moral uprightness – each in accordance with a different principle. The pilot acted as a soldier who is responsible to protect and serve. Tina Geraci displayed a mother's self-sacrificial love for her child. As clergymen, the four chaplains conducted themselves as men called to human service, who acted in obedience to their understanding of what God required of them.

## CONCLUSION

As a mental health professional I have spent many hours with suicidal patients. Over the years, many times I have said, "You will never get my encouragement for you to kill yourself." But then, I have never been with a pilot in a plane bearing down on a schoolyard; a cancer ridden, pregnant woman; or chaplains on a sinking ship. The words you are reading were written in my study, where I was physically and emotionally distant from the six people described in this essay who chose to die that others might live. Any philosophy that does not challenge us to apply it to our own lives is a philosophy not worthy of study. It would please me to die as these six people died. What about you?

*Chapter IX*

# The Significance of
# How People Kill Themselves

## Karl Menninger, M.D.

*Karl Menninger (1893–1990), one of the founders of the Menninger Clinic, is one of America's best-known psychiatrists. The selection below is from his noteworthy book,* Man Against Himself. *In this excerpt he refers to one of his earlier books,* The Human Mind, *in which he argued that psychiatry is a science. Interesting is that a few years before his death, he wrote a letter to another celebrated psychiatrist, Thomas Szasz. Szasz wrote* The Myth of Mental Illness, *in which he argued that psychiatric diagnosis is a medical fraud. In Menninger's letter he apologized to Szasz for declining an invitation to debate with him; implying that upon reflection, Menninger realized that they were not far apart in their opinions.*

> *Razors pain you;*
> *Rivers are damp;*
> *Acids stain you;*
> *And drugs cause cramp.*
> *Guns aren't lawful;*
> *Nooses give;*
> *Gas smells awful;*
> *You might as well live.*
> —Dorothy Parker, "Resume"

In connection with the way in which the need for punishment and the wish to be killed is gratified by suicide we must give some consideration to the significance of the methods used. It is well agreed that, statistically, men appear to prefer shooting and women the taking of poison, gas, or water (drowning). These are obviously related to the masculine and feminine roles in life, i.e. active aggression and passive receptive.

Very suggestive is the consideration of more unusual methods. These illustrate clearly the need for punishment and frequently suggest by the form of punishment, particular erotic values attached to certain symbolic acts. The following excerpt from an article published thirty years ago cannot be excelled for clear exposition of these phenomena:

Nothing is more surprising in the records of suicide than the extraordinary variety and novelty of the methods to which man has resorted to in his efforts to escape the suffering and misfortunes of life. One would naturally suppose that a person who has made up his mind to commit suicide would do so in the easiest, most convenient, and least painful way; but the literature of the subject proves conclusively that hundreds of suicides, every year, take their lives in the most difficult, agonizing, and extraordinary ways; that there is hardly a possible or conceivable method of self-destruction that has not been tried. When I clipped from the newspaper my first case of self-cremation with kerosene and a match, I regarded it as rather a remarkable and unusual method of taking life; but I soon discovered that self-cremation is comparatively common.

I have well-authenticated cases in which men or women have committed suicide by hanging themselves, or taking poison, in the top of high trees; by throwing themselves upon swiftly revolving circular saws; by exploding dynamite in their mouths; by thrusting red-hot pokers down their throats; by hugging red-hot stoves; by stripping themselves naked and allowing themselves to freeze to death on winter snowdrifts out of doors, or on piles of ice in refrigerator cars; by lacerating their throats on barbed wire fences; by drowning themselves head downward in barrels; by suffocating themselves head downward in chimneys; by diving into white-hot coke ovens; by throwing themselves into craters of volcanoes; by shooting themselves with ingenious combinations of a rifle and a sewing machine; by strangling themselves with their hair; by swallowing poisonous spiders; by piercing their hearts with corkscrews and darning needles; by cutting their throats with handsaws and sheep-shears; by hanging themselves with grape vines; by swallowing strips of underclothing and buckles of suspenders; by forcing teams of horses to tear their heads off; by drowning themselves in vats of soft soap; by plunging into retorts of molten glass; by jumping into slaughter-house tanks of blood; by decapitation with homemade guillotines; and by self-crucifixion (Kennan, 1908, p. 227).

Once upon a time such extraordinary methods as these would have been regarded only as indicative of the insane nature of the act of suicide, but that was when we still ignorantly believed that so-called insane behavior had no meaning. The work of Freud and, in this particular direction, the work also of Jung have long since sharpened the eyes and the understanding of psychiatrists to the meaningful nature of every word and act of the psychotic patient. Psychotic behavior is unintelligible to the uninitiated partly because it is so frank, and so clearly and undisguisedly reveals the content of the unconscious. There are, of course, other reasons, one of which is the more archaic type of symbolism used. All human speech is based upon the use of symbolism, but for the most part the symbols are arbitrary and mechanically standardized, whereas the language and behavior of the psychotic patient makes use of more primitive symbols which are unfamiliar in spite of their universality.

We have no right then to dismiss the significance of a particular method of committing suicide as being meaningless. In the light of clinical experience we know with a fair degree of definiteness what some of these symbols, and hence these methods, mean. Let us take, for example, the case mentioned above of suicide by hugging a red-hot stove. Such an act suggests, in addition to the motives which determine the self-destructive act, the existence of a pathologically intense wish to be loved, a feeling of such utter inner coldness that embracing a red-hot stove is like a final climax of destructive satisfaction, as if to say, "At last my heart is warm." One thinks of the humorous popular poem by Service, "The Cremation of Sam McGee," or of the popular song hit of some years ago, "Turn on the Heat." The clinician who works with neurotic patients is so familiar with this complaint that the world is a frigid place, that he will find this less incredible than the practical physician who is more sensitive to external suffering than to internal suffering.

Or again, suicide by self-crucifixion is a quite obvious identification with Jesus, and such Messianic aspirations in less extreme form are not regarded as anything but normal. The teaching in many churches is that one should try to be as much as possible like Jesus and in some forms of religious worship this is carried out, as in the case of Los Hermanos Penitentes of New Mexico, to the extent of a pseudo-crucifixion of the most pious member of the sect. He is fastened to a cross and raised. It is really only a short step from this to a self-appointed and self-inflicted martyrdom of the same sort.

Plunging into molten glass, vats of soap, the craters of volcanoes, etc., represent of course, only more dramatic and more painful forms of drowning. The significance of drowning fantasies was one of the earliest psychoanalytic discoveries, not only because of its frequency as a form of suicide, both contemplated and consummated, but because it is a common fantasy in disguised and undisguised form in the mental life of many people. When subjected to psychoanalytic investigation, such fantasies seem to relate quite definitely to the wish to return to the undisturbed bliss of intra-uterine existence, a kind of reversal of the first great experience of birth. In my book, *The Human Mind*, I give numerous illustrations of this fantasy from the Bible, from poetry, from the casual conversation of man on the street, from the church hymnal, from events in the newspaper, from patients in the sanitarium, and from the writings of Shelley and from Freud.

If the question is asked why the suicide chooses for the drowning such a horrible place, we need only remember that such fantasies may be accompanied by a strong sense of guilt, and there is a well-known (concomitant) conception of the womb, or entry into the womb, as being something terrible. This we recognize in the nature of the mythological representations of entering life hereafter—the dog Cerberus, the terrible river Styx, purgatory, and so on. . . .

To return to the meaning of other methods, allowing oneself to be run over by a truck or steam-roller or train is so closely analogous to submitting oneself in a passive way to an irresistible power, that it may serve as clear and further evidence of the validity of the second component of suicide discussed above (the wish to be killed).

Finally, because of its analogy with the taking of poison and shooting oneself, we should consider the significance of the methods represented by the example of the thrusting of a red-hot poker down the throat. Every physician wonders why some patients who wish to kill themselves with poison do so with such an uncertainly lethal but certainly painful method as drinking phenol. One of these patients calmly drank raw hydrochloric acid; it was vomited, of course; he tried repeatedly thereafter to accomplish suicide with this agent, diluting it with ginger ale. This resulted in a long period of surgical treatment for esophageal stricture resulting from the acid burns, in which it was necessary painfully to dilate the esophagus daily with a bougie. So long as the painful (intra-oral) treatment continued, he seemed quite cheerful and in good spirits, refusing any psychoanalytic treatment as unnecessary. He was finally discharged, re-established his home and business, and then, about a year later, committed suicide successfully by eating fire-crackers.

These methods are very probably related to strong oral cravings . . . i.e., a great intensification of the erotic function of the mouth, connected with a pathological exaggeration of the need for love received in the infantile way i.e., through the mouth. Those familiar with Freud's *Three Contributions to the Theory of Sex* will recognize the psychological relationship of these methods to persistent thumb-sucking in the child or fellatio in the adult. . . .

Just what all these methods may have meant in full detail to these particular individuals we shall never know, but their similarity to neurotic fantasies and dreams with which we are very familiar in psychoanalysis leaves little doubt as to their general significance and reinforces what we have said as to the motives of suicide, viz., that it represents in one act a murder and a propitiation.

## Chapter X

# Professor Bridgman's Suicide

### Sherwin Nuland, M.D.

*Sherwin Nuland teaches surgery and the history of medicine at Yale University. In a* Washington Post *review of the best known of his ten books,* How We Die, *he was described as a, " . . . sensitive observer . . . who has seen much, taken much thought, and written it all down with a superior gift for descriptive narrative." The following excerpt from* How We Die *offers his reflection on suicide in general, and physician-assisted suicide in particular.*

> *Give beer to those who are perishing, wine to those who are in anguish; let them drink and forget their poverty and remember their misery no more.*
> —Proverbs 31:6,7

Taking one's life is almost always the wrong thing to do. There are two circumstances, however, in which that may not be so. Those two are the unendurable infirmities of a crippling old age and the final devastations of a terminal disease. The nouns are not important in that last sentence—it is the adjectives that cry out for attention, for they are the very crux of the issue and will tolerate no compromise or "well, almosts": *unendurable, crippling, final,* and *terminal.*

During his long lifetime, the great Roman orator Seneca gave much thought to old age:

> I will not relinquish old age if it leaves my better part intact. But if it begins to shake my mind, if it destroys its faculties one by one, if it leaves me not life but breath, I will depart from the putrid or tottering edifice. I will not escape from death by disease so long as it may be healed, and leaves my mind unimpaired. I will not raise my hand against myself on account of pain, for so to die is to be conquered. But I know that if I must suffer without hope of relief, I will depart, not through fear of pain itself, but because it prevents all for which I would live.

These words are so eminently sensible that few would disagree that suicide would appear to be among the options that the frail elderly should consider as the days grow more difficult, at least those among them who are not barred from doing so by their personal convictions. Perhaps the philosophy expressed by Seneca explains the fact that elderly white males take their own lives at a rate five times the national average. Is theirs not the "rational suicide" so strongly defended in journals of ethics and the op-ed pages of our daily newspapers?

Hardly so. The flaw in Seneca's proposition is a striking example of the error that permeates virtually every one of the publicized discussions of modern-day attitudes toward suicide—a very large proportion of the elderly men and women who kill themselves do it because they suffer from a quite remediable depression. With proper medication and therapy, most of them would be relieved of the cloud of oppressive despair that colors all reason gray, would realize that edifice topples not quite so much as thought, and that hope of relief is less hopeless than it seemed. I have more than once seen a suicidal old person emerge from depression, and rediscovered thereby a vibrant friend. When such men or women return to a less despondent vision of reality, their loneliness seems to them less stark and their pain more bearable because life has become more interesting again and they realize that there are people who need them.

All of this is not to say that there are no situations in which Seneca's words deserve heeding. But should this be so, the Roman's doctrine would then deserve consultation, counsel, and the leavening influence of a long period of mature thought. A decision to end life must be as defensible to those whose respect we seek as it is to ourselves. Only when that criterion has been satisfied should anyone consider the finality of death.

Against such a standard, the suicide of Percy Bridgman was close to being irreproachable. Bridgman was a Harvard professor whose studies in high-pressure physics won him a Nobel Prize in 1946. At the age of seventy-nine and in the final stages of cancer, he continued to work until he could no longer do so. Living at his summer home in Randolph, New Hampshire, he completed the index to a seven-volume collection of his scientific works, sent it off to the Harvard University Press, and then shot himself on August 20, 1961, leaving a suicide note in which he summed up a controversy that has since embroiled the entire world of medical ethics: "It is not decent for Society to make a man do this to himself. Probably, this is the last day I will be able to do it myself."

When he died, Bridgman seemed absolutely clear in his mind that he was making the right choice. He worked right up to the final day, tied up loose ends, and carried out his plan. I'm not certain how much consideration he

gave to consulting others, but his decision had certainly not been kept a secret from friends and colleagues, because there is ample evidence of having
at least informed some of them in advance. He had become so sick that he felt
it doubtful that he would much longer be capable of mustering up the strength
to carry out his ironclad resolve.

In his final message, Bridgman deplored the necessity of performing his final deed unaided. A colleague reported a conversation in which Bridgman
said, "I would like to take advantage of the situation in which I find myself
to establish a general principle; namely, that when the ultimate end is as inevitable as it now appears to be, the individual has a right to ask his doctor to
end it for him." If a single sentence were needed to epitomize the battle in
which we are all now joined, you have just read it.

No contemporary discussion of suicide, at least one written by a physician,
can skirt the issue of the doctor's role in assisting patients toward their mor-
tality. The crucial word in this sentence is *patients*—not just people, but *patients*, specifically the patients of the doctor who contemplates the assisting.
The guild of Hippocrates should not develop a new specialty of accoucheurs
to the grave so that conscience-stricken oncologists, surgeons, and other
physicians may refer to others those who wish to exit the planet. On the other
hand, any degree of debate about physicians' participation should be wel-
comed if it will bring out into the open a practice that has existed since Aes-
culapius was in swaddling clothes.

Suicide, especially this newly debated form, has become fashionable lately.
In centuries long past, those who took their own lives were at best considered
to have committed a felony against themselves; at worst, their crime was
viewed as a mortal sin. Both attitudes are implicit in the words of Immanuel
Kant: "Suicide is not abominable because God forbids it; God forbids it because it is abominable."

But things are different today; we have a new wrinkle on suicide, aided and
perhaps encouraged by self-styled consultants on the limits of human suffering. We read in our tabloids and glossy magazines that the actions of the de-
ceased are, under certain sanctioned circumstances, celebrated with tributes
such as are usually reserved for New Age heroes, which a few of them seem
to have become. As for the pop culture icons, medical and otherwise, who as-
sist them—we are treated to the spectacle of those publicized peddlers of
death willingly expounding their philosophies on TV talk shows. They extol
their own selflessness even as the judicial system seeks to prosecute them.

In 1988, there appeared in the Journal of the *American Medical Association* an account of a young gynecologist-in-training who, in the wee hours of
one night, murdered—*murdered* is the only word for a cancer-ridden twenty-
year-old woman because it pleased him to interpret her plea for relief as a plea

for death that only he could grant. His method was to inject a dose of intravenous morphine of at least twice the recommended strength and then to stand by until her breathing "became irregular, then ceased." The fact that the self-appointed deliverer had never seen his victim before did not deter him from not only carrying out but actually publishing the details of his misconceived mission of mercy, saturated with the implicit fulsome certainty of his wisdom. Hippocrates winced and his living heirs wept in spirit.

Though American doctors quickly reached a condemning consensus about the behavior of the young gynecologist, they responded very differently three years later in a case of quite another sort. Writing in the *New England Journal of Medicine*, an internist from Rochester, New York, described a patient he identified only as Diane, whose suicide he knowingly facilitated by prescribing the barbiturates she requested. Diane, the mother of a college-age son, had been Dr. Timothy Quill's patient for a long time. Three and a half years earlier, he had diagnosed a particularly severe form of leukemia, and her disease had progressed to the point where "bone pain, weakness, fatigue, and fevers began to dominate her life."

Rather than agree to chemotherapy that had little chance of arresting the lethal assault of her cancer, Diane early in her course had made it clear to Dr. Quill and his several consultants that she feared the debilitation of treatment and the loss of control of her body far more than she feared death. Slowly, patiently, with rare compassion and the help of his colleagues, Quill came to accept Diane's decision and the validity of her grounds for making it. The process by which he gradually recognized that he should help her death is exemplary of the humane bond that can exist and be enhanced between a doctor and a competently terminally ill patient who rationally chooses and with consultation confirms that it is the right way to make her quietus. For those whose worldview allows them this option, Dr. Quill's way of dealing with the thorny issue of assent (since then elaborated in a wise and outspoken book published in 1993) may prove to be a reference point on the compass of medical ethics. Physicians like the young gynecologist, and the inventors of suicide machines, too, have a great deal to learn from the Dianes and Dr. Quills.

Quill and the gynecologist represent the diametrically opposed approaches which dominate discussions of the physician's role in helping patients die— they are the ideal and the feared. Debates have raged, and I hope will continue to rage, over the stance that should be taken by the medical community and others, and there are many shades of opinion.

*Chapter XI*

# Suicide as a Cure for Depression

## Walker Percy, M.D.

*Walker Percy (1916–1990) was a Columbia University trained physician who pursued a career as a writer. After contracting tuberculosis when performing an autopsy, he was sent to a sanitarium to recover. There he read Dostoyevsky and Kierkegaard in preparation for his own work as a philosophical novelist exploring the dislocation of man in the modern age. The following excerpt is from his 1983 nonfiction work,* Lost in the Cosmos: The Last Self-Help Book.

> *All healthy men have thought of their own suicide.*
> —Albert Camus

> *The real reason for not committing suicide is because you always know how swell life gets after the hell is over.*
> —Ernest Hemingway

The suicide rate among persons under twenty-five has risen dramatically in the last twenty years. A recent survey disclosed that the symptom of depression outnumbered all other medical symptoms put together. . . .

*Thought Experiment:* A new cure for depression: The only cure for depression is suicide.

This is not meant as a bad joke but as a serious proposal of suicide as a valid option. Unless the option is entertained seriously, its therapeutic value is lost. No threat is credible unless the threatener means it.

This treatment of depression requires a reversal of the usual therapeutic rationale. The therapeutic rationale, which has never been questioned, is that depression is a symptom. A symptom implies an illness; there is something wrong with you. An illness should be treated.

Suppose you are depressed. You may be mildly or seriously depressed, or suicidal. What do you usually do? Or what does one do with you? Do nothing or something? If something, what is always done is always based on the premise that something is wrong with you and therefore it should be remedied. You are treated. You apply to friend, counselor, physician, minister, group. You take a trip, take anti-depressant drugs, change jobs, change wife or husband or "sexual partner."

Now, call into question the unspoken assumption: something is wrong with you. Like Copernicus and Einstein, turn the universe upside down and begin with a new assumption.

Assume that you are quite right. You are depressed because you have every reason to be depressed. No member of the other two million species which inhabit the earth—and who are luckily exempt from depression—would fail to be depressed if it lived the life you lead. You live in a deranged age—more deranged than usual, because despite great scientific and technological advances, man has not the faintest idea of who he is or what he is doing.

Begin with the reverse hypothesis, like Copernicus and Einstein. You are depressed because you should be. You are entitled to your depression. In fact, you'd be deranged if you were not depressed. Consider the only adults who are never depressed: chuckleheads, California surfers, and fundamentalist Christians who believe they have had a personal encounter with Jesus and are saved for once and all. Would you trade your depression to become any of these?

Now consider, not the usual therapeutic approach, but a more ancient and honorable alternative, the Roman option. I do not care for life in this deranged world, it is not an honorable way to live; therefore, like Cato, I take my leave. Or, as Ivan said to God in *The Brothers Karamazov*: If you exist, I respectfully return my ticket.

Now notice that as soon as suicide is taken as a serious alternative, a curious thing happens. *To be or not to be* becomes a true choice, where before you were stuck with *to be.* Your only choice was how *to be* least painfully, either by counseling, narcotizing, boozing, groupizing, womanizing, man-hopping, or changing your sexual preference.

If you are serious about the choice, certain consequences follow. Consider the alternatives. Suppose you elect suicide. Very well, you exit. Then what? What happens after you exit? Nothing much. Very little, indeed. After a ripple or two, the water closes over your head as if you never existed. You are not indispensable after all. You are not even a black hole in the Cosmos. All that stress and anxiety was for nothing. Your fellow townsmen will have something to talk about for a few days. Your neighbors will profess shock and enjoy it. One or two might miss you, perhaps your family, who will also resent the disgrace. Your creditors will resent the inconvenience. Your lawyers will be pleased. Your psychiatrist will be displeased. The priest or minister or rabbi will say a few words over you and down you will go on the green tapes and that's the end of you. In a surprisingly short time, everyone is back in the rut of his own self as if you had never existed.

Now, in the light of this alternative, consider the other alternative. You can elect suicide, but you decide not to. What happens? All at once, you are dispensed. Why not live, instead of dying? You are free to do so. You are like a prisoner released from the cell of his life. You notice that the door to the cell is ajar and that the sun is shining outside. Why not take a walk down the street? Where you might have been dead, you are alive. The sun is shining.

Suddenly you feel like a castaway on an island. You can't believe your good fortune. You feel for broken bones. You are in one piece, sole survivor of a foundered ship whose captain and crew had worried themselves into a fatal funk. . . .

The consequences of entertainable suicide? Lying on the beach, you are free for the first time in your life to pick up a coquina and look at it. You are even free to go home and, like the man from Chicago, dance with your wife.

The difference between a non-suicide and an ex-suicide leaving the house for work, at eight o'clock on an ordinary morning:

The non-suicide is a little traveling suck of care, sucking care with him from the past and being sucked toward care in the future. His breath is high in his chest.

The ex-suicide opens his front door, sits down on the steps, and laughs. Since he has the option of being dead, he has nothing to lose by being alive. It is good to be alive. He goes to work because he doesn't have to.

## Chapter XII

# Getting a Second Wind

## Rick Reilly

*Rick Reilly's column, "The Life of Reilly," is a weekly feature of* Sports Illustrated. *The bittersweet story of Korinne Shroyer appeared in the September 3, 2007 issue.*

> *It's so wrong, so profoundly wrong, for a child to die before its parents. It's hard enough to bury our parents. But that we expect. Our parents belong to our past, our children belong to our future.*
>
> —Nicholas Wolterstorff

> *My first human act is the recognition of how much I owe everybody else.*
>
> —Thomas Merton

One day five years ago, a bubbly, gorgeous soccer goalie, Korinne Shroyer, came home from the eighth grade, found her father's revolver in his closet and fired a bullet into her skull.

This is about the lives she saved doing it.

Out of a million kids you'd pick Korinne as the last to commit suicide. She was a popular kid in her class in Lynchburg, Virginia. But then she started feeling sad for no reason. Her parents took her to a therapist, who recommended Paxil. But one worry with Paxil is that it can give teenagers suicidal thoughts when they first start taking it. Korinne made it through ten days.

The bullet tore a hole in her father, Kevin, that you could drive an 18-wheeler through. Korinne was Kevin's best friend, the kid who would Rollerblade with him as he ran for hours, the kid who'd come with him to Orioles games and chat with him until his ears hurt. "I used to run all the time," says Kevin Shroyer, 46. "I loved it because it gave me time to think. But [after the suicide], thinking was the last thing I wanted to do."

Kevin, an investigator in the public defender's office, and his wife Kristie, a hairstylist, were able to think one clear and brave and terrifying thought during the six days Korinne survived after the shooting. They decided to send out her organs like gifts.

Her green eyes would go in one direction, her glad heart another, her kidneys still another. Her liver and her pancreas went somewhere else, and her two good lungs—the ones that played the saxophone—went to a Gainsville, Georgia, man named Len Geiger, who was so close to dying that he was practically pricing caskets.

A runner and swimmer and nonsmoker, Geiger suddenly found one day that he had only enough breath for walking and talking, not both. Turns out he had genetic emphysema, also known as Alpha-1, and a lung transplant was his only hope for survival.

He was on his fifth year on the waiting list and "life wasn't worth living," he says, when Korinne pulled the trigger. Geiger received those two young lungs six days later in an operation at the University of Virginia Medical Center.

And that's where the story gets good.

Geiger, now 48, went from 15% lung function to way above average for his age. He got his second wind and second life. He was so grateful, he wrote Korinne's parents to say thank you. And that letter changed everybody's lives.

Korinne's parents wrote back, and Geiger asked to meet, and the next thing you knew Geiger was at a bittersweet gathering that became soaked with every kind of tears.

The Shroyers and their other daughter, Kolby, now 16, gave Geiger a photo album of the girl whose life was now inside him. "She starts out as this beautiful baby," Geiger says. "Then she's a little girl in a Halloween costume. Then a gorgeous teenager. And then the pictures just stop. It was the saddest thing I've ever experienced."

Hours later the group was parting when Kristie said, "Len, can I ask you a favor?" She walked over and stood before him,

"Anything," Geiger said.

"Can I put my hands on your chest for just a second?"

And she stood there, crying, as she felt her dead daughter breathe.

Kevin started to run again. And someone had a great idea. Why didn't he and Len run together? So they did. They ran an 8K together, step for step, next to each other. One man's overflowing joy coming straight from the other's bottomless sorrow.

The whole run, Kevin never shut up. It was so unlike him that, at the end, Geiger asked him, "Why?"

"I had to," Kevin admitted, "because every time there was silence, I could hear Korinne breathing."

Next they ran a half marathon, then a full one. By then, though, the steroids that Geiger had taken for years just to stay alive had damaged most of his joints, and he was running on two artificial hips. The best he could do was race-walk. At the 17-mile mark his hips were screaming. But he refused to quit.

It took six hours and 25 minutes—with Shroyer matching him step by agonizing step—but they finished, hands clasped together, the three of them.

Kevin and Kristie aren't whole yet, but they're getting on with their lives. Geiger, meanwhile, is relishing his. He met a woman, Christina, married her, and they named their first baby Korinne—Ava Corinne. Sometimes he stares at her, awed. "I know that without Korinne, I'm not here today and neither is Ava Corinne."

Sometimes life just takes your breath away, doesn't it?

*Chapter XIII*

# A Suicidologist's Reflections

## Edwin Shneidman, Ph.D.

*Edwin Shneidman, Professor Emeritus at the University of California at Los Angeles and founder of the American Association of Suicidology, is unquestionably a pioneer in suicide research. In the following excerpts from* The Suicidal Mind, *Dr. Shneidman provides an etiology of suicidality drawn from over forty years of investigation, teaching, and clinical work.*

> *To die: to sleep;*
> *No more; and by a sleep to say we end*
> *The heart-ache and the thousand natural shocks*
> *That flesh is heir to, t'is a consummation*
> *Devoutly to be wish'd.*
> —Hamlet (3.1.69–72)

The suicidal act is both a moving away and a moving toward. Psychache, psychological pain, is what the individual wishes to escape; peace is what the person seeks and moves toward. In suicide, the two goals are merged as one: Escape from pain *is* relief—that is how peace is defined. The unbearable pain is transformed into peace; the suffering is taken away. At least, that is what the suicidal person thinks and hopes.

To a suicidal individual, to be unconscious means to be in a state of tranquil quiet, a nothingness and oblivion that is total and complete. Problems are not merely taken care of; there are no problems, and, even better, there is no consciousness of the possibility of problems—or of anything else.

Suicide is an effort to "get away from it all." It is the ultimate escape. . . .

The clinical problem with suicide—the challenge for the potential rescuer—is to wrestle with the fact that the goals of escape and peace *are* beguiling to the suicidal person. If they were not, the person would not be suicidal. One must

46

recognize and deal with the fact that continuance in life is automatically burdened with returns to duty and pain. . . .

Some nonsuicidal people believe that they are pretty much the same as everybody else. But in suicide, there is often the feeling that one's pain is somehow special and greater than the pain and suffering of others, making it unendurable in a special way—bordering on a feeling of grandiosity. This is so because suicidal people tend to cut themselves off from human contact and are talking only to themselves. They think that their suffering and their dying are unique. They imagine their funeral and their mourners—in effect, an existence in this world, at least for awhile, after their own death; that they will be remembered, not forgotten; that they will stay alive in the minds of others. . . .

This book (*The Suicidal Mind*) propounds the view that suicide stems from psychological pain, and that pain comes from frustrated psychological needs peculiar to each person. But the suicidal person must also have the desire or drive to escape the unbearable pain of these frustrated needs. What then is the "psychological soil" in which the suicidal mind malignantly flourishes? While we can agree on the central role of psychache, we must still speculate on the causes of the reactions of the suicidal mind. Are these predilections fostered in early childhood? We know a great deal about the more or less immediate psychological circumstances that surround suicide, but there is no easy answer to the enigma of the "root causes" of a lower threshold for withstanding the psychological pains associated with suicide.

I am totally willing to believe that suicide can occur in adults who could not stand the immediate pain of grief or loss that faced them, independent of a good or bad childhood or good or bad parental care and love. But I am somewhat more inclined to hold to the view that the subsoil, the root causes of being unable to withstand those adult assaults lie in the deepest recesses of personality that are laid down rather early in childhood. . . . One can have one's childhood vandalized. Perhaps—I do not know—every person who commits suicide, at *any* age, has been a victim of a vandalized childhood, in which that preadolescent child has been psychologically mugged or sacked, and has had psychological needs, important to *that* child, trampled on and frustrated by malicious, preoccupied, or obtuse adults. I tend to believe that, at rock-bottom, the pains that drive suicide relate primarily not to the precipitous absence of equanimity or happiness in adulthood, but to the haunting losses of childhood's special joys. . . .

In this book, I have proposed the view that suicide is prevented by changing our perception of the situation, and by redefining what is unbearable. Perceiving that there are other possible ways of seeing things, redefining the impossible, bearing the unbearable, swallowing the undigestible bolus of shame or guilt. . . .

Every single instance of suicide is an action by the dictator or emperor of your mind. But in every case of suicide, the person is getting bad advice from a part of that mind, the inner chamber of councilors, who are in a temporary panicked state and in no position to serve the person's best long-range interests. Then it is time to reach outside your own imperial head and seek more qualified and measured advice from others who, out of their loyalty to your larger social self, will throw in on the side of life, and—to use a Japanese image—will urge the chrysanthemum, not the sword.

All this is consistent with deep beliefs I have held for years. Suicide involves both inner disturbance and the idea of death as an escape. But it is simply good sense not to commit an irrevocable suicide during a transient perturbation in the mind. Suicide is not the thing to do when you are disturbed and your thinking is constricted. There is a short aphorism or maxim that captures this lifesaving truth: Never kill yourself while you are suicidal. You can, if you must, think about suicide as much as your mind wishes and let the thought of suicide—the possibility that you could do it—carry you through the dark night. Night after night, day after day, until the thought of self-destruction runs its course, and a fresh view of your own frustrated needs comes into clearer focus in your mind and you can, at last, pursue the realistic aspects, however dire, of your natural life.

*Chapter XIV*

# Suicide as Psychache

## Edwin Shneidman, Ph.D.

*It is ironic that the ability to experience emotion is an indication of mental health, yet the ability to feel intense pain predisposes one to suicide. In the following essay, Dr. Shneidman elaborates on his five word summary of why people commit suicide: "Suicide is caused by psychache."*

> *Is it nothing to you, all you who pass by? Look around and see. Is any suffering like my suffering that was inflicted on me, that the Lord brought on me in the day of his fierce anger?*
>
> —Lamentations 1:12

As I near the end of my career in suicidology, I think I can now say what has been on my mind in as few as five words: *Suicide is caused by psychache* (sike-ake; two syllables). Psychache refers to the hurt, anguish, soreness, aching psychological *pain* in the *psyche*, the mind. It is intrinsically psychological—the pain of excessively felt shame, or guilt, or humiliation, or loneliness, or fear, or angst, or dread of growing old or of dying badly, or whatever. When it occurs, its reality is introspectively undeniable. Suicide occurs when the psychache is deemed by that person to be unbearable. This means that suicide also has to do with different individual thresholds for enduring psychological pain (Shneidman, 1985, 1992).

All our past efforts to relate or to correlate suicide with simplistic nonpsychological variables, such as sex, age, race, socioeconomic level, case history items (no matter how dire), psychiatric categories (including depression), etc., were (and are) doomed to miss the mark precisely because they ignore the one variable that centrally relates to suicide, namely, intolerable psychological pain; in a word, psychache.

By its very nature, psychological pain is tied to psychological needs. In general, the broadest purpose of most human activity is to satisfy psychological needs. Suicide relates to psychological needs in that suicide is a specific way to stop the unbearable psychachical flow of the mind. Furthermore, what causes this pain is the blockage, thwarting, or frustration of certain psychological needs believed by that person (at that time and in those circumstances) to be vital to continued life.

Suicide is not adaptive, but adjustive in the sense that it serves to reduce the tension of the pain related to the blocked needs. Murray's (1938) monumental volume *Explorations in Personality* provides a comprehensive list of psychological needs, and their definitions: abasement, achievement, affiliation, aggression, autonomy, counteraction, defendence, deference, dominance, exhibition, harmavoidance, infavoidance, sentience, succourance, and understanding.

There is an integral relationship between suicide and happiness—or rather the absence of it. Genuine happiness—contrary to the 19th and 20th century materialistic notions that narrowly identified happiness with the mere absence of pain and the presence of creature comforts—has a special magical quality (Spender, 1988). There is a mundane happiness of comfort, pain avoidance, and psychological anesthesia. But genuine, magical happiness has relatively little to do with creature comfort; rather, it is the kind of ecstasy and consuming exuberance that one can experience only in a benign childhood. To the extent that suicide relates to happiness, it relates in people of any age—not to lack of mundane happiness but the loss of childhood's magical joys.

The prevention of suicide (with a highly lethal person) is then primarily a matter of addressing and partially alleviating those frustrated psychological needs that are driving a person to suicide. The rule is simple: Mollify the psychache.

In the progression to suicidal outcome, I believe we can distinguish seven components. They are:

a) the vicissitudes of life; those stresses, failures, rejections, and catabolic and social psychological insults that are omnipresent by virtue of living.
b) various approaches to understanding human behavior. Suicidal behavior (as is all behavior) is obviously multidimensional, which means, in practice, that its proper explication has to be multidisciplinary. The relevant fields for suicidology include biochemistry (and genetics), sociology, demography, epidemiology, psychology, psychiatry, linguistics, and so on. The reader should appreciate that *this* paper is limited to the psychological approach to suicide, without derogating the importance of other legitimate approaches.

c) the vicissitudes of life as they are perceptually funneled through the human mind and apperceived (or appreciated) as ecstatic, pleasurable, neutral, inconsequential, or painful. If there is extreme psychache, a necessary condition for suicide is present. "I hurt too much."

d) the perception of the pain as unbearable, intolerable, and unacceptable; another necessary condition for suicide, in addition to psychache. "I won't put up with this pain."

e) the thought (or insight) that cessation of consciousness is the solution for the unbearable psychache, still another necessary condition. In a phrase, death is preferable to living, with death as a means of egression or escape. "I can kill myself."

f) a lowered threshold for enduring or sustaining the crippling psychache, a final necessary condition for suicide. A priori, people with more or less equal amounts of psychache might have radically different thresholds for tolerating or enduring psychological pain. (In life, pain is ubiquitous and inescapable; suffering is optional.)

g) the suicidal outcome. "I hurt too much to live." . . .

Here, finally, after over forty years of experience as a suicidologist, is a tight summary of my current beliefs about suicide.

1. The explanation of suicide in humankind is the same as the explanation of the suicide of any particular human. Suicidology, the study of human suicide, and a psychological autopsy (of a particular case) are identical in their goals: to nibble at the puzzle of human self-destruction.

2. The most evident fact about suicidology and suicidal events is that they are multidimensional, multifaceted, and multidisciplinary, containing, as they do, concomitant biological, sociological, psychological (interpersonal and intrapsychic), epidemiological, and philosophical elements.

3. From the view of the psychological factors of suicide, the key element in every case is the psychological pain: psychache. All affective states (such as rage, hostility, depression, shame, guilt, affectlessness, hopelessness, etc.) are relevant to suicide only as they relate to unbearable psychological pain. If, for example, feeling guilty or depressed or having bad conscience or an overwhelming unconscious rage makes one suicidal, it does so only because it is painful. No psychache, no suicide.

4. Individuals have different thresholds for enduring or tolerating pain; thus, the individual's decision not to bear the pain—the threshold for enduring it—is also directly relevant.

5. In every case, the psychological pain is created and fueled by frustrated psychological needs. These needs have been explicated by Murray (1938, pp. 142–242).

6. There are modal psychological needs with which the person lives (and which define the personality) and there are vital psychological needs whose frustration cannot be tolerated (which define the suicide). Within an individual, these two kinds of needs are psychologically consistent with each other, although not necessarily the same as each other.

7. The remediation (or therapy) of the suicidal state lies in addressing and mollifying the vital frustrated needs. The therapist does well to have this template (of psychological needs) in mind so that the therapy can be tailor-made for that patient. Often, just a little bit of mollification of the patient's frustrated needs can change the vital balance sufficiently to save a life.

## Chapter XV

# I Want to Die

## Rod Steiger

*The late actor, Rod Steiger (1925–2002), appeared in over one-hundred mo-
tion pictures. He was a three-time Academy Award nominee, earning the
award for best actor for his 1967 portrayal of Sheriff Bill Gillespie in "The
Heat of the Night." Not wanting to glorify war, he turned down the role of
General George Patton—the role for which George C. Scott earned the Academy Award for best actor.*

*Steiger suffered through an eight-year clinical depression from 1976 to
1984. In the midst of this "hellish existence," as he characterized it, he wrote
the following essay, read at the Carter Center Mental Health Conference. A
mere reading of it cannot do justice to the powerful dramatic reading he presented at the conference.*

> *I am the most miserable man living. If what I feel were distributed to the whole
> human family, there would not be one cheerful face on earth. Whether I shall
> ever be better, I cannot tell; I awfully forbade I shall not. To remain as I am is
> impossible; I must die or be better, it appears to me.*
>
> —Abraham Lincoln (January 23, 1841 letter
> to his law partner William Herndon)

I want to die. I don't want to live. I have no feeling for movement. To be
left alone; to disappear; not to be bothered with washing, shaving, talking,
walking, going to the bathroom. Just to get out of this tunnel and the heavy
darkness, cold and oily, constantly pressing against my brain; gray-faced, un-
shaven, dirty of body, empty of mind.

Acting? What the hell is so important about acting? Oh, Lord—the para-
lyzing fear of not being able to remember my lines . . . the projections, the
images, constant visions of failure. They're watching, they are watching! I

can feel their eyes all over my skin. It's time to act! And the crew is waiting—
thirty of them. The director's watching; my partner in the scene is watching;
a rat in the corner of the saloon of the studio set is watching.

I must not scream, I must not scream in front of them. I must not—I must
not listen to what's left of my mind. I must not run; I must not run. They're
going to find out that I'm weak. They'll find out I'm in pain.

Oh, God . . . what God?

I'll break down; I'll look like a fool, an idiot, and they'll find out . . . I can't
act!

But wait . . . there is a way out. You get a gun—a nice, cool gun. And then
. . . wait a minute . . . I don't want to have a mess. I'm worried . . . I'm worried about the mess. I'll leave behind the head half gone; the blood on the
wall, the flowers, the carpet, all over the cat. I don't want my loved ones to
walk in on that.

There's a way, there's a way. I live by the beach. Yes, and it's waiting . . .
yes it is—the moving, relentless ocean. I'll get a small rowboat and when my
wife's in town doing business and my daughter's in Europe so she won't
know 'til later, I'll row out into the ocean. I'll lower myself over the side of
the boat, holding tightly with my right hand (because I'm left-handed). And
then, keeping my head and shoulders above the water, holding in my left hand
the gun, I'll point it toward the sky and then I'll lower the gun, taking the bar-
rel in my mouth and PULL THE TRIGGER!

Then, I'll rest . . . I'll rest. And then the boat floats away and my body floats
in the other direction . . . no mess . . . no mess . . . fish food!

Strange, isn't it? I'm more worried about the mess than taking my life.
Death, you do not frighten me! But, lingering does. Let it not be a long stretch
of dying. Let me not linger. Let me in the depths of my depressive sleep,
never-ending, in that darkness—depart.

Let me die simply. Not wake up—that's exciting, that's a goal; that would
be an accomplishment.

I feel the cold sheets of fear moving about my body. If I don't move . . . if
I don't move . . . if I don't breath . . . maybe they will absorb me.

And then me, in never-ending sleep . . . sleep . . . I rest . . . I rest.

*Chapter XVI*

# I'm Dying

## William Styron

*William Styron (1925–2006) had established himself as an exceptional novel-
ist with* Lie Down in Darkness, The Confessions of Nat Turner, *and* Sophie's
Choice *when at age sixty he was stricken with a clinical depression. In* Darkness Visible: A Memoir of Madness, *he described his "despair beyond despair" which once moved him to say to a passing stranger in a restaurant,
"I'm dying." He addresses the inadequacy of the clinical term "depression"
in the following excerpt from his memoir.*

> *There is but one truly serious philosophical problem, and that is suicide. Judg-
> ing whether life is or is not worth living amounts to answering the fundamental
> question of philosophy.*
>
> —Albert Camus

When I was first aware that I had been laid low by the disease, I felt a need,
among others things, to register a strong protest against the word "depression." Depression, most people know, used to be termed "melancholia," a
word which appears in English as early as the year 1303 and crops up more
than once in Chaucer, who in his usage seemed to be aware of its pathological nuances. "Melancholia" would still appear to be a far more apt and evoca-
tive word for the blacker forms of the disorder, but it was usurped by a noun
with a bland tonality and lacking any magisterial presence, used indifferently
to describe an economic decline or a rut in the ground, a true wimp of a word
for such a major illness. It may be that the scientist generally held responsible for its currency in modern times, a Johns Hopkins Medical School faculty
member justly venerated—the Swiss-born psychiatrist Albert Meyer—had a
tin ear for the finer rhythms of English and therefore was unaware of the se-
mantic damage he had inflicted by offering "depression" as a descriptive

noun for such a dreadful and raging disease. Nonetheless, for over seventy-five years the word has slithered innocuously through the language like a slug, leaving little trace of its intrinsic malevolence and preventing, by its very insipidity, a general awareness of the horrible intensity of the disease when out of control.

As one who has suffered from the malady in extremis yet returned to tell the tale, I would lobby for a truly arresting designation. "Brainstorm," for instance, has been unfortunately preempted to describe, somewhat jocularly, intellectual inspiration. But something along these lines is needed. Told that someone's mood disorder has evolved into a storm—a veritable howling tempest in the brain, which is indeed what clinical depression resembles like nothing else—even the uninformed layman might display sympathy rather than the standard reaction that "depression" evokes, something akin to "So what?" or "You'll pull out of it" or "We all have bad days." The phrase nervous breakdown seems to be on its way out, certainly deservedly so, owing to its insinuation of a vague spinelessness, but we still seem to be saddled with "depression" until a better, sturdier name is created.

The depression that engulfed me was not of the manic type—the one accompanied by euphoric highs—which would have most probably presented itself earlier in my life. I was sixty when the illness struck for the first time, in the "unipolar" form, which leads straight down. I shall never learn what "caused" my depression, as no one will ever learn about their own. To be able to do so will likely forever prove to be an impossibility, so complex are the intermingled factors of abnormal chemistry, behavior and genetics. Plainly, multiple components are involved—perhaps three or four, most probably more, in fathomless permutations. That is why the greatest fallacy about suicide lies in the belief that there is a single immediate answer—or perhaps combined answers—as to why the deed was done.

The inevitable question, "Why did he (or she) do it?" usually leads to odd speculations. Reasons were quickly advanced for Abbie Hoffman's death: his reaction to an auto accident he suffered, the failure of his most recent book, his mother's serious illness. With Randall Jarrell it was a declining career cruelly epitomized by a vicious book review and his consequent anguish. Primo Levi, it was rumored, had been burdened by caring for his paralytic mother, which was more onerous to his spirit than even his experience at Auschwitz. Any one of these factors may have lodged like a thorn in the sides of the three men and been a torment. Such aggravations may be crucial and cannot be ignored. But most people quietly endure the equivalent of injuries, declining careers, nasty book reviews, family illnesses. A vast majority of Auschwitz survivors have borne up fairly well. Bloody and bowed by the outrages of life, most human beings still stagger on down the road, unscathed by real depression. To discover why some people plunge into the downward spiral of depression, one must reach beyond the manifest crisis—and then still fail to come up with anything beyond wise conjecture. . . .

What I had begun to discover is that, mysteriously and in ways that are totally remote from normal experience, the gray drizzle of horror induced by depression takes on the quality of physical pain. But it is not an immediately identifiable pain, like that of a broken limb. It may be more accurate to say that despair, owing to some evil trick played upon the sick brain by the inhabiting psyche, comes to resemble the diabolical discomfort of being imprisoned in a fiercely overheated room. And because no breeze stirs this caldron, because there is no escape from this smothering confinement, it is entirely natural that the victim begins to think ceaselessly of oblivion.

## Chapter XVII

# In Control of Our Death

## Judith Viorst

*Few writers have the demonstrated versatility of Judith Viorst. Trained as a psychoanalyst, she has authored eight collections of poetry and five works of prose. Her children's books include* Alexander and the Terrible, Horrible, No Good, Very Bad Day. *Her acclaimed psychological work,* Necessary Losses, *was a bestseller.*

> *In a sense, and as in melodrama, killing yourself amounts to confessing. It is confessing that life is too much for you or that you do not understand it.*
> —Albert Camus

> *They tell us that suicide is the greatest piece of cowardice . . . that suicide is wrong; when it is quite obvious that there is nothing in the world to which every man has a more unassailable title than to his own life and person.*
> —Arthur Schopenhauer

Several years ago a friend and I arranged a lunch date with a distinguished elderly man who had just moved to town, a man who seemed quite unhappy with his new home and the new conditions of his life. My friend and I didn't know him well and I had met him only once, but in asking him out we were not simply being kind. For the man was Bruno Bettelheim, the brilliant and controversial child psychologist, and we anticipated an interesting afternoon. It never happened.

The morning of our date, when we put in a call to arrange a time to pick him up, we were informed that he was unavailable. We called again and received the same reply. Later that day we learned that Dr. Bettelheim would be permanently unavailable. He had killed himself.

Not knowing the state of his mental or physical health, I have no opinion on why Bruno Bettelheim chose to end his life. But an arrogant fantasy lingered long in my head. If only he'd waited for lunch . . . If only we three shared a nice afternoon . . . If only we'd then made plans for another date, and then for another date after that. . . . If only, then maybe . . .

Lacking the information, our quite human response to suicide is that there are better ways to fix "it," to feel that something could have been done to make that terminated life worth living. But in fact I agree with those who believe in the concept of rational suicide. I agree with those who believe that there are times when it makes sense to do ourselves in. I also believe, however, that we are entitled to make that choice (or to ask for assistance in carrying out that choice) only under certain stringent conditions.

We must be in the terminal phase of a devastating illness, or unmanageably, insupportably disabled.

The decision to die must originate with us, and we must be competent to make it. We obviously will be sad, but our decision should not be distorted by a depression that may be transient and reversible.

All efforts must be exhausted to control our intractable pain, to make our daily living conditions tolerable, and to rectify whatever careless, callous, or demeaning health-care practices are breaking our spirit and grinding down our soul.

Before we choose to kill ourselves we must understand that death is the end—forever—of living in this world of music and lilacs, sunrise and sunset, the taste of fresh bagels, the touch of someone we love. Before we choose to kill ourselves we must understand that we're dead for a very long time. We must know with absolute clarity exactly what—and why—it is we're leaving. We must know that there is no other way to fix it.

I'll grant that all the above is almost unreasonably rational. But it seems to me it ideally should be the only kind of suicide we should support.

In a process a German psychiatrist, Alfred Hoche, has characterized as "balance-sheet suicide," we can weigh the pros and cons of living and dying. But even the strongest advocates of such balance sheets would preclude the option of suicide for the young, recognizing their tendency to see their sorrows and setbacks as unendurable, recognizing their readiness to seek an ultimate remedy in death.

A thirty-four-year-old woman, clearly contented with every aspect of her life now, wrote a letter responding to a newspaper article on "self-deliverance." It said: "Ten years ago . . . I attempted suicide several times, sincerely believing that death was the 'only satisfactory release.' I thank God I did not have access then to any guides to supposed self-deliverance. . . . Please . . . give other people a chance to have a new life in *this* world."

Her point was echoed in a letter sent to the *Journal of the American Medical Association* by two child psychiatrists and a clinical social worker who voiced strong objections to a book on suicide, maintaining that its "lurid examples, explicit instruction and vigorous advocacy . . . may have an especially pernicious effect on adolescents." Considering the 1991 survey of 11,631 high-school students found that in the previous year *one out of twelve* had attempted suicide, we must, in any justification of suicide, remember the vulnerability of the young.

It takes a lot of years, a lot of experience, and a lot of common sense to be the kind of bookkeeper who can weigh the pros and cons of living and dying. But although it seems clear that balance-sheet suicide isn't meant for kids, it also seems clear that for certain adults, under certain conditions, suicide may be a legitimate choice.

There is surely nothing like a suicide for asserting control, for taking control, of our death.

Charlotte Perkins Gilman, a distinguished writer and feminist, ended her life at the age of seventy-five, explaining in her suicide note that "I have preferred chloroform to cancer." She also left a manuscript defending suicide as a release from "the suffering and waste we now calmly endure," noting that "the record of a previously noble life is precisely what makes it sheer insult to allow death in pitiful degradation."

Sixty years later, in 1995, Earl Blaisdell of Falls Church, Virginia, chose not to *live* in pitiful degradation. Eleven years of multiple sclerosis had left him almost a hundred pounds thinner. He could move only his face and neck and left hand. He was bedeviled by chronic bedsores. He was starting to go blind. He no longer had control of his bladder and bowels. Earl wanted out.

But Carmi, his wife, had already refused to help him with an overdose. His doctor had refused to help with an overdose. And his efforts to locate the famous suicide doctor, Jack Kevorkian, had failed. And so, one day, having finished a buttered slice of seven-grain bread, he announced to his disbelieving wife, "I want you to know I've just eaten my last meal." Forty days later, surrounded by his family, Earl—age fifty-seven—died of starvation, having killed himself in the only way he still retained the power to do.

In a tape he made in secret, to be given to his family after he died, Earl forcefully defends his desperate decision:

> I know you folks are trying to convince me that I should stay alive. But if you were layin' in this bed like this, you wouldn't do it either. . . . If I can find a way to get out of here, I'm going to try to find it. . . . I don't want to exist anymore . . .I'm going through hell. . . . Don't feel bad about me being gone. I'm plain better off.

One year later Earl's wife and Elaine and Michael, his two grown stepchildren, were struggling to make peace with the way he died. But she said she understood why Earl chose suicide. She said that "he was finally in control."

Michael was willing to grant that Earl showed "strength and a lot of will," but he nonetheless felt that "he took the coward's way out." He said that he "respected his choice" but added, "I don't respect the way he died."

Some—I among them—would say that the only thing wrong with Earl Bliasdell's suicide was that he hadn't been able to do it more easily.

# References

## FOREWORD

Bateson, M.C. 1990. *Composing a life*. New York: Grove Press.

## PREFACE

Camus, A. 1955. *The myth of sisyphus*. New York: Vintage.

## INTRODUCTION

Szasz, T. 1973. *The second sin*. New York: Doubleday and Co.

## CHAPTER VIII

Churchill, W. June 4, 1940. Speech to the House of Commons.
Durkheim, E. 1894. *La Suicide: etudie de sociologie*. Paris, France: Alcan.
Jamison, K.R. 1995. *An unquiet mind*. New York: Random House.
King, M.L. Recovered from *About.Com Classic Literature* on January 21, 2008.
Myers, D. 1992. *The pursuit of happiness: who is happy and why*. New York: William Morrow.
Rand, A. 1991. *The virtue of selfishness*. New York: Penguin Books.
Robinson, D. 2007. "Great ideas in philosophy: lecture number 50." Chantilly, VA: The Teaching Company.

*The American heritage dictionary*. 1973. New York: The American Heritage Publishing Company.

*The Washington Post*. March 7, 1995. "Mother picks death to continue life through son."

# CHAPTER X

Kennan, G. "Problems of suicide." *McClure's Magazine*. Volume XXXI, p. 227.

# CHAPTER XIV

Murray, H. (1938). *Explorations in personality*. New York: Oxford University Press.

Shneidman, E.S. (1985). *Definition of suicide*. New York. Wiley.

Shneidman, E.S. (1992). "A conspectus of the suicidal scenario. In R.W. Maris et al (Eds.) *Assessment and prediction of suicide*. New York: Guilford.

www.ingramcontent.com/pod-product-compliance
Lightning Source LLC
Chambersburg PA
CBHW021823270326
41932CB00007B/317